Beating Combat Stress

Beating Combat Stress

101 Techniques for Recovery

John Henden

WILEY-BLACKWELL

A John Wiley & Sons, Ltd., Publication

Library of Congress Cataloging-in-Publication Data

Henden, John.
   Beating combat stress : 101 techniques for recovery / John Henden.
       p. cm.
   Includes bibliographical references and index.
   ISBN 978-0-470-97480-3 (pbk.)
1. Post-traumatic stress disorder.   2. Veterans–Mental health.   I. Title.
   RC552.P67H45 2011
   616.85'21–dc22

                                        2010035696

A catalogue record for this book is available from the British Library.

Set in 14/16 pt Times by Toppan Best-set Premedia Limited
Printed and bound in Singapore by Fabulous Printers Pte Ltd

1   2011

Dedication

I dedicate this book to the hundreds of thousands of servicemen and women from all four armed services who have served in the frontline of various theatres of operations over the last few hundred years. The vast majority, as others will in the future, simply dust themselves off before making the necessary readjustments, at their own pace and in their own time. Some will have needed help from comrades, the chain of command, their regimental association, family welfare workers, or other agencies to complete that adjustment. This handbook is dedicated particularly to those servicemen who have found it tough on their return; or who have experienced symptoms later on. It may be used as a manual for welfare workers who are providing the most effective help possible, and as a self-help guide or "buddy-aid" for all service personnel who have need. Service wives or partners, parents or other relatives may find it helpful too, in discovering the widest range of valuable tools and techniques. Theories about what might be helpful for service personnel with combat operational stress reaction (COSR) can be found in many textbooks and papers. This handbook contains no theories; instead, it is a practical how-to-do guide, packed with field-tested tools and techniques that work in the majority of cases.

If there are three lead messages within this handbook, they are as follows:

- to get serving troops back to maximum operational fitness and health as soon as possible
- to promote early intervention, wherever and whenever possible, for all service personnel who have been on tours of duty, anywhere in the world

- to equip both serving personnel and veterans with the widest range of tools and techniques to promote a life lived well.

Contents

About the Author

John Henden
BA(Hons), RMN, Dip.Couns. (Univ. of Bristol), MBACP

John Henden is a former soldier, therapist and trainer of military welfare workers within all four armed services.

John is an acclaimed international author, conference presenter and solution-focused trainer. He is a regular presenter at European Brief Therapy Association conferences and was a founder member of Solutions in Organisations Link-up. Over the last 10 years, he has worked in over 15 countries.

He has worked in health, welfare and support services for over 30 years, having gained both a deep knowledge and a wide experience of "what works", when it comes to helping individuals get their lives back on track. Throughout his career in health and welfare, he has never lost sight of the potential in people to make the necessary changes to live useful and productive lives, despite any earlier labels they may have been given.

Foreword

The conflicts in Iraq and Afghanistan have thrust into view tragic images of fallen servicemen and women returning home in flag-draped coffins, and heightened public awareness of the need to support those who have suffered life-changing injuries. Those with longer memories may recall the Falklands Campaign of 1982: British television screens filled with pictures of severely burned Welsh Guardsmen struggling off the stricken Sir Galahad or 2 PARA burying their dead at Goose Green. But those whose injuries we see are just a small proportion of those who suffer in the course of duty. Far more numerous are those who suffer through the stress of what they have experienced, and their injuries are invisible to all but themselves and their close families and friends. In past generations these wounds would have gone unrecognised and untreated, but not anymore.

John Henden, an ex-serviceman, therapist and trainer in the military welfare field, is at the forefront of the fight to transform those who suffer from the stress of combat back to being the fully effective soldiers and citizens they once were and, he argues with great conviction, have always been. This practical, no-nonsense book will make a tremendous contribution in this vital area. Anyone who picks it up will realise at once that there is no "psychobabble" here, just soldier-focused common sense.

One of the biggest obstacles to treating those brave individuals who, in previous generations, were likely to have been dismissed as suffering from some sort of "shell shock", was simply admitting that their reaction was normal. Yes, for them it was unpleasant, worrying and severely depressing, but it is now widely accepted that this is a perfectly normal reaction to situations of great stress. Like any illness it needs to be recognised, accepted and treated. The military's "macho" culture has often sought to stigmatise those who sought help, but that is increasingly a thing of the past. Few soldiers who have experienced combat can deny they have felt fear, and no one can be certain how they will react the next time. The military community has reached a level of operational competence and professional maturity where it is now fully recognised that all mates in difficulty need help, whether they are bleeding visibly or hurting inside. We understand these things so much better today.

I am sure that this book will make a major contribution to heading off psychiatric injury at an early stage; the practical advice is both simple to understand and wise in substance. Moreover the six sections are divided up in such a way that the subject matter is readily accessible; the reader gains instant benefit from turning the pages. One only wishes others would write and speak in such clear terms. There is nothing to be gained by pretentious language and academic mumbo jumbo; Henden's communication skills are a lesson in getting a message over with crystal clarity. He introduces readers to the concept of Triggers – random events which can set off unwelcome memories producing debilitating Flashbacks, but he quickly dissolves these scary moments into something that is normal and can be handled with the application of his reassuring strategies. In the sections that follow, he offers similar techniques to deal with Unwelcome Thoughts, "The Lows", the desire to live Life to the Full, and Sleep Disturbance. The latter is so common that his practical tips will benefit not just those suffering with combat stress, but anyone struggling with the pressures of our overheated society.

Over and above the book's principal sections, Henden includes nine appendices which underpin all that has gone before. He lifts the veil on his own Solution Focused Brief Therapy, and goes on to provide important signposts for those working in this life-restoring area for the benefit of others. Throughout, while the military focus is evident, it is not applied in such a way that prevents relevance to other walks of life. This will significantly widen the appeal and the success of this invaluable book.

Henden has consulted widely, thought carefully, and offers compelling advice in an area of life that has become much more open to receive it. In this regard he is a man for our times, and this book is a most welcome product. If used as intended, hope will be restored and many lives transformed.

General Sir Richard Dannatt GCB CBE MC DL

Former Chief of the General Staff

July, 2010

Preface – The Book's Purpose

During the 18 years or so in which I have worked with survivors of all sorts of extreme experiences, I have been struck by the shortage of appropriate help. Often, where this help has been available, it has been of the wrong sort; practitioners have had limited skills; or service users have found it difficult to engage.

Many pamphlets, booklets and leaflets, designed to provide help for both clients and their relatives and friends, have fallen short with regard to specific ideas and techniques for recovery. This has been the case, particularly for service personnel.

The various textbooks aimed at helping practitioners tend to concentrate on background, awareness, theories and statistics, rather than getting down to specifics on what might be useful. Those books that do list tools and techniques do not describe very many; are over-complicated or wordy; and appeal more to highly educated practitioners. This comprehensive handbook is intended to plug this gap in provision, with its many tools and techniques from which to choose.

The book's twin purpose is both to provide a handbook for practitioners and at the same time to be a self-help book or buddy-aid manual. Regarding other books available for the self-help market, there are two I would endorse, which may be read in addition to this one. The first of these is by Armstrong, Best and Domenici (2006) and is entitled *Courage after Fire: Coping Strategies for Troops Returning from Iraq and Afghanistan and Their Families*. This is good particularly in regard to tips and techniques for strengthening mind and body; and for coming to terms with changed views of others, self and the world.

The second book is by Charles Hoge (2010), *Once a Warrior, Always a Warrior: Navigating the Transition from Combat to Home*. The noteworthy strengths of this book are how to deal with the many and various emotions on return from theatre; and how partners and family members can be most helpful.

Those servicemen who have developed reactions to their experiences "on tour" may need help in various ways. The six sections of this handbook are intended to cover all these experiences.

Is this book about "post-traumatic stress disorder" (PTSD)? As mentioned again later, in Section 5, the PTSD label is easy for some practitioners to apply, but difficult for the serviceman to remove. From the solution-focused perspective, PTSD has negative connotations, with ideas of hopelessness and permanence. Seeing PTSD, then, as an unhelpful and outdated term, and using combat operational stress reaction (COSR) instead, breathes "ideas of hope, optimism, temporariness and normality into the situation" (Moore and Reger, 2007, p. 166).

Most of us, at some time or other during our lives, experience reactions to one sort of stress or another. This is life. We acknowledge the stress; think of how we might reduce it; what needs to happen to bring it to an end; and then take action. Time alone, in many instances, will see a lessening of it. The reaction some may have to combat operational stress need not be seen as much different from this.

The majority of the 101 techniques and strategies within this handbook are easy to understand and apply, by both service personnel and veterans themselves. Spouses, partners, relatives and friends will find the same. For practitioners and welfare workers, a basic counselling skills qualification is recommended; and even a preferred therapeutic approach is desirable. This is especially the case with Eye Movement Desensitisation and Reprocessing (EMDR) and the Rewind Technique, where expert professional assistance should be sought.

This book has been written and published for informational purposes, and is not intended to serve as a substitute for therapy or treatment of any specific disorder. The author and publisher are offering information and advice for consideration, but, ultimately, each serviceman or veteran (and spouse, partner, buddy or family member) needs to seek out and find whatever works best for him. This book is not intended to be a substitute for professional help when it is needed.

There are so many good news stories to tell about how different reactions to combat operational stress have been resolved. But there are all too many, still, where the opposite is true: either because the practitioner has insufficient knowledge about the tools and techniques

within the pages that follow, or because the serviceman
does not know where to find the best self-help technique.

Please take as much as you need from this handbook and pass on the good news!

Acknowledgements

I would like, first, to acknowledge Royal Marine WO1 Ian Robbins, who several years ago encouraged me to develop a two-day training package to equip military welfare workers better in their work with personnel returning from operational theatre. Without delivering these many workshops across all the armed services, and the many conversations and discussions which were had, this handbook might not have been written.

I am grateful, too, to Gail Morris of the Army Welfare Service, whom I have known in her various capacities within that valued service, over the past 10 years or so. At a difficult stage in the development of the handbook, she was able to provide suggestions and ideas to give the project renewed life, and to ensure its publication.

I want to thank Darren Reed, Commissioning Editor of Wiley-Blackwell, who listened with great interest to my original ideas for this book and, believing it to be a virtuous project, gave me appropriate guidance along the way.

My thanks go, too, to David and Pat Hopewell, who were kind in letting me use their Bristol flat, with inspirational views across the city and the hills of North Somerset beyond. Most of the manuscript was written there, over several stays.

I am grateful, as ever, to my wife Lynn who has been very understanding of my need "to go away and write". She has on many occasions been most patient in her role as "wordsmith's widow".

I am grateful to Dr Alasdair Macdonald for his encouragement and support with this project, over some three or four years. This came first in the form of enlightening articles, and then in the form of useful books loaned. Latterly, help with the research base for solution-focused brief therapy (SFBT), as outlined in Appendix A, was much appreciated.

I would like to thank Dr Harry Procter for casting his eye over later drafts of the manuscript, and for making some useful suggestions on both design and content. His quick grasp of both structure and content, and his clarity of thinking, are always appreciated.

My search for an illustrator ended when I remembered Keith Rainer, who had helped me with a previous important project. Thanks, Keith, for all the drawings provided for the various sections within the book.

The person to whom I reserve my deepest gratitude for, in putting the whole handbook together, is Alison Wright, my secretary. She has steadily and patiently word-processed each redrafting of the manuscript over many months. A big "thank you" for this sterling work.

Finally, I would like to thank the many serving service personnel and veterans, whom I have worked with over many years, both in a personal and a professional capacity. Also, I am grateful to the many civilian clients who have survived road traffic accidents (RTAs), near-death experiences, armed robberies and other traumatic events. It is on both military and civilian clients that the tools and techniques in this handbook have been field-tested, by me and others over many years, with both encouraging and amazing results.

Introduction

In the following pages there are over 100 tools and techniques that have been found helpful to thousands of returning service personnel especially over the past 50 years or so. The emphasis is on simplicity and effectiveness, with a minimum of jargon and absence of "psychobabble", wherever and whenever possible.

If you are a worker or practitioner (welfare worker, counsellor, therapist, psychiatrist, psychologist, medical officer or doctor, help-line worker), you will find this manual an invaluable addition to your "toolbox" for when working with all sorts of returnees from various theatres of operations and other deployments. Your fellow practitioners have been using and field-testing the following tools and techniques for years. The practice-based evidence continues to accumulate; and, more importantly, the personal testimonies of personnel who have been involved in carnage of one sort or another or other "incidents", have regained control and gone on to live relatively trouble-free and fulfilling lives. As practitioners, we have both an ethical responsibility and a duty of care to undertake this work. The outcomes for service personnel when workers avoid getting involved in this work, or use inappropriate treatments, can be unsatisfactory at best; and, at worst, tragic. Testimonies of people in this group are all too numerous to mention. Sadly, in the past, some of our colleagues have said, "He needs to be referred to a specialist", or "I don't want to take him on in case I make things worse" and "I don't know what I can offer him" as ways to avoid getting involved. What follows in the pages ahead will not only give great confidence to workers but also provide the fullest range of tools and techniques to get down to the job in hand and be of maximum effectiveness. If you need inspiration and encouragement right now, it may be helpful to read Appendices A–I before continuing.

If you are a returnee from a recent deployment, you may be interested in testing out one or several of the tools and techniques within this handbook, whether or not you consider yourself in need, it may be a helpful manual for you, personally. Or you may like to read through these pages on behalf of a comrade who, at the moment, is having a few difficulties in some way or another. "Buddy-aid" is both powerful and effective and you may be surprised how helpful you can be.

You may have survived a recent (or not so recent) RTA, and are affected still by some thoughts and images or avoidance reactions. This manual will give you what you need, to lay these thoughts, images and feelings to rest.

It may be that you had someone who died or was killed or maimed before your very eyes. You, too, may find this manual helpful. If you are a survivor of a near-death experience (a "near miss", perhaps), where you think frequently about what might have occurred, this manual is for you, too.

For serving personnel and ex-serving, it takes courage and resolve, to pick up this handbook and thumb through its pages to see what may be helpful or useful for either yourself or others. It does not mean you have "gone soft"; are "weak"; or in some way are a lesser person than you were. Indeed often quite the opposite is the case. By following some or many of the suggestions made, in the sections that follow, you will become even stronger and more resilient than you are right now. You can look forward to living a fuller and more satisfying life. You will be in a better position to help comrades, former comrades and others who may have need. Where a sense of guilt, fear and anxiety may be present, you will replace this with a sense of renewed direction and purpose in life. Section 6 is particularly useful as a personal or individual workbook, giving both encouragement and inspiration as it is completed.

You will have noticed that the text within the handbook is more generously spaced and of a larger point size than usual. This is to make it more user-friendly. Also, for the same reason, it is illustrated with various drawings of military hardware and personnel. If, as a veteran, one or other of these drawings acts as a trigger for an experience (or experiences) you had in theatre, there follows a number of tools and techniques you can use to deal with them.

When trying out the many tools and techniques within the six sections of the handbook, if one or other does not work for you or your client, it is not about "failure". It means, simply, that the tool or technique does not suit you or your client, and that you need to try another. This fits well with a basic principle of the solution-focused approach: "going with what works".

Incidentally, I have used the male pronoun throughout the book so, for serviceman, read serviceman/ servicewoman; for he, read he/she; and for his, read his/hers.

How to Use This Handbook

You will find that the tools and techniques within the handbook are laid out under six main sections:

1. Triggers
2. Flashbacks
3. Unwelcome Thoughts
4. "The Lows"
5. Sleep Disturbance
6. Living Life to the Full

For best results for workers to use in their sessions – go simply to the section that applies. Within each section, often the term "horses for courses" applies. Some personnel find one tool or technique particularly helpful; others will experiment with another that proves helpful. All are available to try: it is often about finding "what works". The case studies will be helpful too.

Section 6 is a workbook that can be used by both workers and servicemen themselves, but is aimed specifically at the serviceman. Pages may be photocopied as many times as necessary to be used personally, or to be passed around to comrades and friends. The workbook may also be used in "buddy-aid".

Section 1
Dealing with "Triggers"

1. "That was then, this is NOW … !"
2. "This is normal …"
3. "Breathe it away …"
4. Welcoming triggers through "mindfulness"
5. The 5-4-3-2-1 method

A trigger is something (e.g., a sight, sound, smell, taste or bodily sensation) that sets off a reaction, taking you back to a particular event or situation. Triggers are highly unpredictable. Fearing and fleeing from triggers *does not work*. It is better to face them and deal with them. So instead of going for avoidance – go for acceptance. Dealing with them takes out their sting, and enables us to remain in control. Also, it prevents the trigger developing into a "flashback" (see Section 2).

The strong suggestion in this manual is not to run from or try to avoid triggers, but to *welcome* them. This allows us to take control, practise the

Beating Combat Stress: 101 Techniques for Recovery. By John Henden.
© 2011 John Wiley & Sons Ltd.

necessary techniques and to gain mastery over them. The result is often (surprise, surprise!) that the triggers occur less often and, when they do occur, are dealt with easily and effectively. Welcoming them enables us to expose ourselves to events or situations, in a way that's not harmful.

The Tools and Techniques

1. "That Was Then, This Is NOW ... !"

This technique is very powerful for arresting a trigger in its tracks. It ensures the locus of control remains with the serviceman and not with the trigger, which could easily lead into a flashback.

The secret is to practise saying **"That was then, this is NOW ... !"** on a regular basis, so that it is ready to use in an instant. It is important for workers to encourage service personnel to slow down their pace of speech, lower their tone of voice and say the sentence *forcefully*, with the emphasis on the "NOWWWW ... !"

With this technique held in readiness, triggers – which are highly unpredictable – need not be feared; instead, they may be *welcomed*.

"Bring on the triggers!"

One service user, who was traumatised over a number of years, has reported that, on average, he encounters one trigger roughly every two weeks, but that this is now not a problem. By using this technique for just a few seconds on each and every occasion, he continues to live life to the full, regardless. He added that he looks forward to the triggers occurring, so he can both practise and prove to himself that the technique works.

"The smell of the pork ribs"

An infantryman, who had been involved in an incident where several comrades had been badly burned, said that, as a result, he avoided going to barbecues. He found the smell of the cooking meat – especially where pork ribs had been provided – just too much to bear.

Clearly, he had been missing out on many potentially enjoyable family and other social gatherings, for a few years.

However, although being able to avoid barbecues to which he had been invited, he could not avoid the smell of neighbours' barbecues, wafting across his back yard.

By learning and practising "That was then, this is NOWWWW ... !", in addition to accepting invitations to others' barbecues, he proved he had gained full control of his trigger by holding one of his own.

2. "This is Normal ..."

Another way to gain mastery over a trigger is to train the service user to say quietly and firmly to himself, "THIS IS NORMAL ..." Instruct him, as soon as the trigger is observed, to become consciously aware of it; to see it for what it is; and to say to himself, "This is normal. These experiences occur from time to time. I am noticing it fully. And it will pass." In addition to this statement being so simple and easy to learn, it has great reassurance value.

"Gunfire – no problem"

A soldier, who had returned from a six-month tour of Afghanistan, happened to be walking his dog along a riverside path, well out in the country. Suddenly, he heard the sound of short bursts of machine-gun fire from an army barracks in the distance. Naturally, thoughts of Afghanistan entered his head rapidly, and in particular a sticky situation his platoon was in on one particular occasion. He was able to prevent this trigger developing into a full-blown flashback by calmly and firmly saying out loud, "This is normal. I am bound to hear the sound of gunfire or other similar sounds from time to time, when I am out and about."

3. "Breathe It Away ..."

This is another powerful technique for gaining control over triggers. Often triggers can lead to a serviceman taking a sharp in-breath. As I will describe, this technique enables people to maintain control by controlling their breathing. As a welfare worker or practitioner, you can provide the following instruction:

When the trigger occurs, take control first by naming the experience (sight, sound, smell, taste, bodily sensation) as a trigger. Then slowly breathe out, using your diaphragm (this means ensuring your stomach goes in on the out-breath, and out on the in-breath).

This is easy. Breathe in, slowly and gently, for the count of 7 (ensuring that your stomach goes out on the in-breath). Then, breathe out, for the count of 11. It is known as "the 7/11 technique". Practise this for a couple of minutes about six or seven times a week, over a period of six to eight weeks. This ensures it is bedded in fully as a technique for you to use at any time. It is worth practising this type of breathing under normal circumstances anyway, when no triggers are in sight. Not only will you be ready for the trigger when it occurs, but you will feel good, generally. This type of breathing is widely recommended for people who want to get control back for themselves, on occasions when they are feeling out of control.

"Breathing away loud bangs"

A former sailor, who had served on a destroyer that had taken a direct hit from an Exocet missile, was affected by any loud crash or bang. Most often, it would be a vehicle back-firing, objects being thrown into a metal skip or an up-and-over garage door slamming.

After regular practise, he was able to switch instantly the sharp in-take of breath into a slow out-breath, then follow the 7/11 breathing routine just described.

4. Welcoming Triggers Through "Mindfulness"

This fits well with replacing avoidance with acceptance, as outlined in the introduction to this section.

The technique counters powerfully the "fight or flight" response by disarming it. This is how it works:

At the first whiff of a trigger, say "Ah. I recognise you!", "Welcome!" etc. This response is the complete opposite to trying to run from it or push it down or away. Simply acknowledge the trigger and how you feel about it right now. There is no need for the brain and the body to become activated, ready for a fight, for it will pass. Once you have welcomed it, use the techniques 1, 2 or 3 described earlier.

5. The 5-4-3-2-1 Method

This method is very useful for dealing with triggers, pulling the serviceman back to the here and now. (Also, it is good for inducing sleep if woken at night by internal or external events: see Section 5.)

Service personnel may be instructed as follows:

"Open your eyes.
Notice five things that you can see.

Close your eyes.
Notice five things that you can hear.
Notice five things that you feel in your body (e.g., warmth, pillows; not emotions).

Open your eyes.
Notice four things that you can see.

Close your eyes.
Notice four things that you can hear.
Notice four things that you feel in your body.

Open your eyes.
Notice three things that you can see.

Close your eyes.
Notice three things that you can hear.
Notice three things that you feel in your body.

Open your eyes.
Notice two things that you can see.

Close your eyes.
Notice two things that you can hear.
Notice two things that you feel in your body.

Open your eyes.
Notice one thing that you can see.

Close your eyes.
Notice one thing that you can hear.

Notice one thing that you feel in your body."

Repeat if necessary (it often requires two repetitions to induce sleep, see Section 5).

After using the exercise four or five times, it will become easier and the calming effect will be greater.

Section 2
How to Deal with Flashbacks

1. "Shrinking" (or "the Reversing Technique")
2. Dual Awareness
3. The "Stop!" technique and "Replaying the DVD" later
4. The Rewind Technique
5. Confront the flashback, head-on
6. Voluntarily, bring on a pleasant flashback
7. Eye Movement Desensitisation and Reprocessing (EMDR)

Definition of a flashback: "A recurrence of a memory, feeling or perceptual experience from the past" (American Psychiatric Association, 2000).

Flashbacks, which are normal, are recollections from the past. They may be pictures, sounds, smells or feelings, or the lack of them (a kind of numbness). Unless we deal with them effectively, as they arise, flashbacks can cause us to feel trapped, powerless, and/or out of control. We may feel at the mercy of our experiences. ***This need not happen***, as will be seen in the following pages.

The tools and techniques for dealing with flashbacks are easy to learn and easy to teach.

Beating Combat Stress: 101 Techniques for Recovery. By John Henden.
© 2011 John Wiley & Sons Ltd.

Flashbacks can be pleasant. We can induce them voluntarily and consciously. We do this by calling up memories of the past in the form of sight, sound, touch, taste, smell. A case example of this can be seen below.

There follows a good selection of techniques to deal with flashbacks into unpleasant experiences. What is of fundamental importance is to arrest the flashback in its tracks and to minimise its effects.

The Tools and Techniques

1. "Shrinking" (or "The Reversing Technique")

The "shrinking" technique is a powerful and effective way to tackle flashbacks in cases where the experience is one of incoming missiles, of whatever type. It has been used most effectively for military personnel who have had battlefield experiences of this order; and for vehicle drivers involved in serious RTAs, where debris from other vehicles or complete vehicles themselves have come towards them at speed.

The effectiveness of this technique, like so many others, is attributable to the regaining of power and control. Instead of the distressing psychological and physical sequence of events that might be experienced, take control and "dispose" of the incoming missile in a novel, safe and more comfortable way. Over time, this reduces the severity of the flashback's effects until it has no power left at all.

The technique is easy for practitioners to teach, and easy for service personnel to learn by themselves.

The instruction for the technique is as follows:

"What I invite you to do is to visualise the missile coming towards you. As it approaches you are able to get a good look at it …   At the moment before impact, in your mind's eye …   stop the missile in its tracks …   Now send it back in a different direction towards the distant *horizon*. As it travels this new path, *change its colour to any colour* you choose …   As it travels further away, notice how much smaller it gets …   until it becomes a mere speck on the horizon. If you keep watching, you will notice you cannot see it any longer."

"It is important to practise this at least three times a week for about six weeks. If, on some weeks, you manage two practice sessions instead of three, that is okay. Notice the ways in which you find it helpful or useful."

Some service personnel, after practising this technique on a number of occasions, rename it "the reversing technique", which is fine.

"The car wreckage missile – sorted"

An experienced driver of 40-ton, 6-axle lorries, who was also a former serving soldier, was involved in a fatal RTA, in which three car passengers in two separate vehicles were killed.

A car, which had been overtaking him, crashed head-on into the path of an oncoming lorry, some 40 yards distant. The impact speed was in the region of 110–120 mph. A front wheel of the overtaking car, with attached steering parts, flew through the air at great speed towards the driver's windscreen, hitting it with a giant "thwack!" before bouncing off and away. Triggers into flashbacks of this event for this driver were seeing windscreens of passing lorries and department store windows bulging slightly, caused by doors opening and closing, traffic passing, or the wind.

On the one hand, the driver dealt with the triggers by "That was then, this is NOW … !"; on the other, he practised the "shrinking" technique at a regular time each day for a few weeks. This enabled him to have control over the trigger; and, should the full flashback to the accident occur, he could have control over it by changing it in the way just outlined. The result was that the flashbacks were less severe and less frequent. They stopped altogether after about four to five months.

2. Dual Awareness[1]

This powerful technique has the following instructions. When teaching it to

[1] Adapted from a protocol drawn up by Babette Rothschild (2003).

service personnel or learning it yourself, make sure you say the words slowly, deliberately and with a strong voice:

"It seems we have got two things going on here. **Right now** I am feeling (isolated/lonely/fearful/etc.)[2] and I am

sensing in my body ... (three or so things: i.e., heart racing, perspiring, tremulousness, etc.)[3]

They are real sensations – that's what I am experiencing right now – because I am remembering the firefight/explosion/ incident/RTA/hold-up/accident, etc.[4]

However, at the same time, I am looking around here where I am now (the place/room[5] where I am now) and:

I can see five things ...   (name them)

I can hear five things ...   (name them)

I can sense the following five things ...   (name them)

And so I know the firefight/explosion/incident/RTA/hold-up/ accident/etc.[6] is not happening now or any more."

[2,3,4,5,6]Delete the words which do not apply to you, adding others as appropriate.

"Fireworks: where did they come from!"

A veteran of the first Gulf War was walking through his local park one summer's evening, as a "prom in the park" was coming to its closing stages. A few minutes later, for him all hell seemed to break loose as the firework display began with a flash and a bang.

Immediately, he had the beginnings of a full-blown flashback of being in Saudi Arabia, where an incoming Iraqi SCUD missile exploded into a hangar, a few dozen yards from him.

He applied the **"Dual awareness" technique**, as follows:

"It seems we have got two things going on here. **Right now** I am feeling terrified and am sensing in my body my heart racing, eyes wide and alert, tightening of my stomach, and sweaty hands. I am wanting to run and take cover.

They are real sensations – that's what I am experiencing right now – because I am remembering the SCUD missile attack all those years ago.

However, at the same time, I am looking around where I am here in the park and:

- I can see five things:
  - the orchestra playing
  - the smiling, delighted faces of the audience

○ the beautiful colours of the fireworks

○ the moon, partially covered by clouds, and

○ the grass looking everywhere quite a deep dark green.

- I can hear five things:
  ○ the whoosh of the rockets, as they rush heavenwards
  ○ the pleasant sound of some violins
  ○ the chatter of groups of friends gathered watching
  ○ the clinking of bottles with wine glasses, and
  ○ the distant hum of the evening traffic.
- I can sense the following five things:
  ○ the smell of the firework smoke
  ○ the gentle breeze on the side of my face
  ○ my shoes against the soft turf of the park
  ○ the sulphurous taste of the smoke, and
  ○ my left thumb struggling to get out through the hole in my glove!

And so I know the SCUD attack in Saudi Arabia is not happening now or any more."

Once the exercise had been completed, the veteran wandered on, taking in the atmosphere of both the concert and the fireworks, having regained his composure and sense of control.

3. The "Stop!" Technique and "Replaying the DVD" Later

This technique is very powerful for dealing both with flashbacks and other regularly occurring unwanted thoughts.

Jointly, it addresses the issues of "control" or "boundarying". With certain flashbacks, there may or may not be a definable trigger: the person is back into the situation of discomfort in an instant. They feel out of control and at the mercy of the flashback or unwanted intrusive thought. They have no way of predicting how and when they occur, feeling they have no control over them. There are no boundaries to the experiences. They can occur any time during waking hours: from the very point of waking until last thing at night, as they drift off into sleep. First, we need to encourage the serviceman to take control. This is done by asking them to wear a rubber band on a wrist of their choosing. The rubber band should be neither too tight nor too loose. The ideal diameter is that of the red ones that postal workers drop accidentally on the pavements! However, the ideal band is not of the same width as these: the thin variety is preferred, because it produces a more painful sting on the inside of the wrist when pinged.

Once applied to the wrist, the serviceman is invited to practise pinging the rubber band. (It is more effective if the practitioner demonstrates this with his own band first, so that he models the experience of the pain)

The instructions are as follows:

i.   As soon as the flashback or intrusive thought occurs, reach for the rubber band, and ping it against the inside of your wrist; at the same time, say "Stop!"
ii.   As you say "Stop!", you are saying to yourself "I will give the incident some thinking time later."
iii.   Carry on with whatever you were doing or thinking about before the flashback occurred.
iv.   Continue using the "Stop!" technique throughout the day, however many times the flashback occurs.
v.   At a time in the early evening (at least two hours before you go to bed), spend half an hour "replaying" the

incident, as if you were watching it all on a DVD. Begin at a point where all was safe, peaceful and quiet before the incident. Then, go through each aspect of the incident, to its end, and then to the point where safety, peace and quiet was restored.

NB: It is important to "replay the DVD" at least two hours before retiring to bed, so that you can be involved in other thoughts and activities before bedtime. This minimises the risk of the flashback's contents being worked out in dreams or nightmares.

vi. Repeat this every day. Use the "Stop!" technique whenever the thoughts occur; and follow it up in the evening with the "replaying of the DVD".

There have been some amazing results achieved with this twin technique. Flashbacks have been reduced from around 80–90 per day down to 5–6 per week, within about 6 weeks.

While clients may be keen to spend a full half hour on the "replay" stage later, eventually they find they need less time, and anyway it becomes boring.

While some reddening of wrists occurs in the early days, the need to use "Stop!" lessens as the brain learns it gets punished when thinking about the incident.

"Surviving the reaction to an IED"

Three Royal Marines had been walking along a track towards a rocky outcrop after "Position clear!" had been given. Suddenly an explosion from an improvised explosive device (IED) sent them somersaulting into the scrub. One was killed outright and a second lost a forearm and a lower leg in the incident. The third (the service user) had blast scarring, a neck injury and developed hearing problems.

One month after the incident, being troubled by up to 70 flashbacks a day, and having nightmares, he came to the Royal Marines Welfare Service for help. (He had heard about someone else in the battalion who had been helped.)

The welfare worker demonstrated the technique, instructing the marine to go away and practise it.

Ten days later, at the second session, the marine said his flashbacks were now much more under control, being down to about five to seven a day. Also, he said he was sleeping much better, having fewer nightmares.

With the "replaying of the DVD" part of this technique, more power can be provided by adding in "the paper strips method". The instruction for this runs as follows:

i. Fold five sheets of A4-size white paper into half, horizontally.
ii. Press hard along the crease with your thumbnail, before tearing the five sheets in half. This provides two lots of five (now A5 size).
iii. Fold each new set of A5 sheets in half, again horizontally.

iv. Repeat as before, tearing along the crease.

v. Continue this process until you have 40 (5 × 8) strips of paper.

vi. Then fold two sheets of coloured A4-size paper, horizontally.

vii. Continue tearing, folding and tearing, until these two sheets have produced 16 strips.

viii. Now, with Step v above, "replay" the original incident, beginning with what you were doing before it began.

ix. With each part of the story, place on a table one white strip.

x. Place a coloured strip each time you remember something you did well; a personal quality/strength/characteristic that you brought into play; or something you were pleased about.

xi. Continue the process, right through the incident and on to the point where equilibrium was restored, or a point of safety was reached.

xii. You should end up with a giant multi-layer paper strip sandwich of both the white and coloured paper strips. Usually, personnel end up using white strips to coloured strips to a ratio of about 4:1.

There is a threefold purpose to adding in the paper strips method to this technique:

i. It reduces the risk of re-traumatisation, because strengths, qualities and other positive points punctuate the story.

ii. It empowers service users, because they are taking more control of the story while they "replay the DVD" to themselves.

iii. It speeds up the time when boredom will occur for the service user. The brain will, literally, become fed up with having to go through this exercise day after day, and will be wanting to be occupied with something else more interesting.

This "Stop!" technique, and "replaying the DVD" later, has been highly effective in reducing flashbacks and unwelcome thoughts for many people.

It is best illustrated by the following example.

A three-tonner lorry driver was travelling along a bending section of un-dualled by-pass when he noticed a motorcyclist travelling towards him. Being a motorcyclist himself, he thought that the rider was going too fast for the bend, and that his positioning on his side of the road was not good.

The lorry driver slowed to about 40 mph, hoping the motorcyclist would slow down too. Within seconds, he saw the rider's terrified expression as he hit the front of the cab at an impact speed of in excess of 90 mph. For about a week after the incident, the driver was having 70–80 flashbacks per day. Adding the paper strips method to "replaying the DVD", the exercise went as follows:

- "There I was driving along the open road, at a steady 50 mph."
  - ○ Lay down one white strip (WS).
- "The sun was shining and there were a few puffy white clouds in the sky."
  - ○ WS
- "I was listening to a play on Radio 4; and, being mid-p.m., there was not much traffic about."
  - ○ WS
- "I could see a motorcyclist at about 200 yards away, coming towards me. He seemed to be going too fast for the curve."
  - ○ WS

- "I slowed down to about 40 mph, as he continued to approach at speed."
  - lay down one green strip (GS)
- "He was still coming fast into the curve and his road positioning and 'lean' were all wrong."
  - WS
- "He was coming straight towards my cab; I braked sharply and safely, slowing fast."
  - GS
- "I saw his terrified expression and he seemed to be mouthing the words 'Oh God!'."
  - WS
- "There was a terrific bang and a jolt to my cab. I travelled a bit further, scraping wreckage until I brought the three-tonner to a halt."
  - WS
- "I put the lorry into gear, applied the handbrake, turned off the ignition, picking up my mobile phone and stepped down from the cab."
  - GS
- "I took a quick look at the mangled bike wreckage and the dead rider. He was beyond help."
  - WS
- "I phoned 999, giving them an accurate position of the incident."
  - GS
- "Other vehicles had slowed down and stopped."
  - WS
- "Already there was one driver, directing traffic."
  - WS
- "I informed the other drivers and passengers, who were approaching, to stay away from the front of the lorry, for their own benefit. There was nothing to be done for the driver; and the emergency services were on their way."
  - GS
- "Another two drivers agreed to direct traffic."
  - WS
- "I returned to my cab, to phone my transport manager, to inform him of events."
  - GS

- "I switched the radio over to a music channel, to try and calm my nerves, while waiting for the emergency services to arrive."
  - GS
- "The police arrived first."
  - WS
- "I got down from the cab and locked it behind me, in accordance with my driving rules."
  - GS
- "I sat in the police car and made a statement."
  - WS
- "I noticed the ambulance arrive. They removed the body."
  - WS
- "As the policeman was finishing his interview, I heard a fire and rescue tender arrive, at the same time that the breakdown vehicle joined the scene."
  - WS
- "I returned to the cab to remove all personal items and my company documents that may have been under the dashboard."
  - GS
- "I had a lift in the police patrol car back to my home."
  - WS
- "On the way, the policeman said his colleague would be at the scene for some time, measuring skid marks on the road, etc."
  - WS
- "On the way, the policeman chatted, reassuringly. He was a kind bloke and gave me a cup of hot, sweet tea from his own flask."
  - GS
- "He told me that he sees too many motorcycle fatalities in the course of his work."
  - WS
- "Once home, I had a hot bath. I chucked in loads of bath salts and lay there for about an hour-and-a-half."
  - GS
- "I dressed and went downstairs to the kitchen. All I could eat was a bowl of soup and some dry bread."
  - GS
- "I sat in my lounge, trying to watch some TV, before going to bed."
  - WS

4. The Rewind Technique[7]

The rewind technique should be learned and practised under the guidance of an experienced practitioner and works in around 90% of cases. It is carried out in a state of deep relaxation or trance.

Once relaxed, clients are asked to recall or imagine a place where they feel totally safe and at ease. This is a special place. Their relaxed state is then deepened. They are asked to imagine that, in their special place, they have a TV set and a DVD player with a remote control facility. Next, they are asked to float to one side of themselves, out-of-body, and watch themselves watching the traumatic event on the TV (this is a means of creating significant emotional distance). Then they are asked to rewind the trauma, as if in real life. Then, they relive it as if in real life (this sets up the "kinaesthetic visualisation"). The film begins at a point before the trauma occurred – a point of safety – and ends when the trauma is over and they feel safe again. They then float back into their body and imagine pressing the video-rewind button, so that they see themselves very quickly going backwards through the trauma, from safe point to safe point. Then they watch the same images, but going forwards very quickly, as if pressing the fast-forward button.

All this is repeated back and forth, at a speed dictated by the individual concerned and as many times as needed, until

[7]This technique was developed by Richard Bandler, of Neuro-Linguistic Programming (NLP) fame. He, in turn, got it from Milton Erickson, who invited clients to look at themselves inside a crystal ball. Griffin and Tyrrell (2004) have developed the idea into an even more powerful form.)

the scenes evoke no emotion. They are asked to go forwards and backwards about four times, which seems to be sufficient in dealing with the traumatic memory, in most cases.

If it is desirable to instil confidence for facing the feared circumstance in the future – for instance, driving a car or using a lift – they are asked to imagine a scenario in which they are doing so, and feeling confident and relaxed. Once accomplished, clients are brought out of trance, and the work or the rewind technique is complete.

Besides being safe, quick, painless and side-effect free, the technique has the advantage of being non-voyeuristic. Intimate details do not have to be voiced. It is the client who watches the "film", not the worker.

5. Confront the Flashback, Head-on

If, on this occasion, you have not succeeded in identifying and dealing successfully with the trigger, say to yourself the following:

"Okay, so this is a flashback, but I know deep down, the worst is over because the feeling and sensations I am having are in the past. I am here, now, in the present, so let's get the control back!"

Four simple steps to do this are:

i.   Pinch yourself, or press one foot on top of the other.
ii. Breathe normally, over-emphasising the out-breaths and in-breaths.
iii. Breathe on the out-breath to the count of 11; and on each in-breath to the count of 7.
iv. Re-establish yourself in the present by using the five senses:

- I can see five things …
- I can hear five things …
- I can feel five things …
- I can taste or smell five things …

Notice in which particular ways you are regaining control.

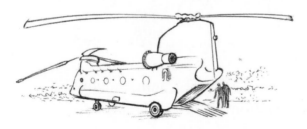

6. Voluntarily, Bring on a Pleasant Flashback

We have all got a wonderful collection of fond or happy memories from the past, whether these come from early childhood, teenage years or more recently. This is a good opportunity to prove you can be in control, at will. Bring on one of these pleasant flashbacks by a particular sight, memory, smell, taste or sensation. By doing this for ourselves, we are then more able to describe its benefits and to be able to teach it to others.

"The sweet perfume of roses"

An aircraftsman in the Royal Air Force, who had had an unhappy childhood, remembered a regular summer holiday staying in a small guest-house, in a coastal resort.

The proprietor's main passion was to cultivate rare varieties of garden rose. The aircraftsman seldom missed an opportunity to take a deep nose-full of scent from them. Over many years recently, he had allowed himself to sniff garden roses, as he walked by various properties.

He enabled the trigger (the roses' scent) to develop into a full-blown flashback: the many happy holiday times of his childhood at the seaside.

7. Eye Movement Desensitisation and Reprocessing (EMDR)

This form of treatment has helped hundreds of thousands, worldwide, who have suffered from a wide range of trauma, including combat operational stress reaction (COSR).

EMDR involves stimulating eye movement in such ways that the brain's information-processing systems are stimulated. Amazingly, negative internal messages are squashed instantly, while the person's eyes flicker back and forth, side to side, while focusing on the painful memory.

The instructions for the service user are as follows:

i.   I want you to sit comfortably in front of me.
ii.   Now, for about a minute, shift your eyes rapidly from side to side, while focusing on the incident. Use a closed fist with two fingers up in a V sign, about a foot in front of you, to help keep your eyes on track.
iii. Continue this pendulum action with your hand for the full minute, focusing fully on the incident.
iv.   Towards the end of the minute, picture mentally the worst part of the incident. Now focus on the worst part of the incident, while continuing to shift your eyes in the lateral position.
v.   With the image clearly in focus and eyes rotating, feel your entire body engulfed in panic.
vi.   Take full account of how your discomfort is spreading from top to bottom and allow it to flow freely, without resisting.
vii. Now, stop the anxiety abruptly, by taking a deep breath.
viii. Stop the mental image.
ix.   Focus on the left and right movement of your two fingers, concentrating on them fully.
x.   You will notice, hypnotically, that you will feel less anxiety and be more entranced in pacing your eyes as your two fingers shift back and forth.
xi.   Repeat this method several times, bringing to mind other painful fears about the incident.
      NB: Some warnings about EMDR. With some personnel, there is a risk of

dizziness with this technique. So those who get dizzy easily are not advised to use it. Often this technique can be very effective in removing symptoms in the short term, but they can resurface again unexpectedly, later on. You will then need to repeat the exercise. Like all the tools and techniques in this handbook, this is another for your toolbox, for you to try out.

Section 3

How to Deal with Unwelcome Thoughts

1. "Tackle the guilt trip"
2. "Tell it – don't bottle it"
3. "Get in some 'de-grimming' or black humour"
4. "The letter from the future"
5. "Changing the mind-set"
6. "How to beat the 'If only ...' monster on the shoulder"
7. "Write, read and burn (or write, read and shred)"
8. "Park it ...   and move on ..."
9. "Let it go ...   Let it go ...   Let it go ..."
10. "Fast-forwarding the DVD of your life"
11. "Ways to deal with anger build-ups"
12. Change your mental attitude to the unwelcome thoughts
13. Visualisation
14. The solution-focused feelings tank

Unwelcome (or intrusive or unwanted) thoughts are common in all people. They are thoughts that find their way, often repeatedly, into our everyday thinking. They may take the form of "flashbacks" mentioned earlier, or simply be irritating and annoying interruptions into whatever we are doing at the time. They can prevent us from having happy and fulfilling

Beating Combat Stress: 101 Techniques for Recovery. By John Henden.
© 2011 John Wiley & Sons Ltd.

lives. In order to stop them causing us emotional or psychological distress, we must deal with them effectively.

Service personnel must be encouraged to take control and to deal with unwanted thoughts, effectively.

Below are many useful tools and techniques for helping service personnel to combat these unwanted thoughts. They will then be able to get on with whatever activity they are involved in, with little or no disturbance.

The Tools and Techniques

1. "Tackle the Guilt Trip"

A common unwelcome thought in many survivors of combat trauma is guilt. Statements that keep intruding into the waking mind are: "I feel so guilty because I survived and he died"; "Things went wrong and I am to blame"; "I feel so bad about it and it's all my fault!"; "The contact went badly wrong, but if only I had …   it wouldn't have happened!", etc.

When disturbing things like this have happened to us, it is quite normal to have these unwelcome guilt thoughts. It is often referred to as "survivor guilt".

There are two ways to deal with these.

i. **"It was not your fault"**

First, tell yourself it was not your fault or you are not to blame. In most situations, even though we do feel guilty, when we look at the hard facts, we discover we are not to blame and in no way was it our fault. Give the incident or situation a reality check.

"Lucky escape from an RPG"

A serviceman told a welfare worker about an incident where an incoming rocket-propelled grenade (RPG) hit a building within a secure compound. He had been working in the building with a comrade when the RPG struck, demolishing the building. His comrade was killed outright but he survived, on account of his being confined in the toilet at the time.

The serviceman came into the welfare worker's office, as if "wearing sackcloth and ashes", feeling full of remorse. The incident had happened some six months ago. He said, "I feel so guilty. Sam took the full force of the hit and I got off scot-free because I was in the bog, taking my time in there. I should have gone too."

The welfare worker helped him look at the facts:

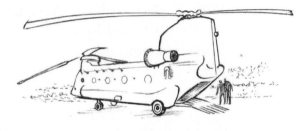

- He had no control of the trajectory of the RPG.
- It was quite by chance that he, and not his buddy, had been in the toilet.
- When the noise had stopped, he went out to see if there was anything he could do to save him. Sam would have done the same for him.
- We have no control, in many instances like this one, over who will be taken out by effective enemy fire; or when.
- No one can ask more of us than our best, in any set of circumstances we find ourselves in.

A final question seemed to have great impact:

"What strengths, qualities and skills did you bring to the fore to help you get through that ordeal?"

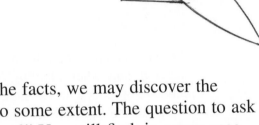

Over the following two sessions, the guilt seemed to fade away.

ii. "You are not wholly to blame"

In some situations or with some incidents, after taking a long hard look at the facts, we may discover the serviceman was to blame, to some extent. The question to ask is, "Were you 100% to blame?" You will find, in every case, the answer is "no", because there is always someone else to share it.

This is illustrated best with the following example.

"Guilt shared is more than halved"

Alec, a young section commander in a recent conflict was racked with guilt over a patrol he was leading that went wrong, leading to the death of a highly valued comrade. The mission was to check out some derelict buildings for an insurgents' arms dump. He had assumed the enemy were not in the area, so had not taken all necessary precautions. His experienced comrade was scouting out in front as the patrol approached the buildings. Immediately a shot rang out, his comrade taking a hit through his left eye. Since the incident, Alec had been on leave, was drinking heavily and was unable to return to his unit. He was stuck firmly in the statement: "Spikey is dead, and it is all my fault!"

With the help of the welfare worker, Alec was able to see he was not 100% to blame. It is true, he should have been more cautious, *but* who else should shoulder some of the blame? With the welfare worker's help, he came up with the following and their approximate percentages of total blame:

The insurgent sniper	30%
The politicians back home	30%
Spikey	20%
Local military intelligence	20%
His platoon commander	15%
Other members of his section	10%
Total for "others":	125%

This happens often, where the tot-up of the others' percentages exceeds 100%. It can only be 100% in total, *including* Alec's percentage. So pressing Alec, to take a share of this 100%, helps him get a realistic percentage of his part in the incident.

Once Alec had accepted his share, he believed he should carry approximately 30% of the blame. He could then deal with that, learn from it and move on.

2. "Tell It – Don't Bottle It"

Bottling up, suppressing or pushing down has never done anyone any good in the long run. True, it can be helpful, while an operation is ongoing, because it enables fighting troops to get on effectively and efficiently with the job in hand.

However, afterwards, if we push things down for any length of time, they will bubble up in the daytime when we are least expecting them; or surface at night in the form of vivid dreams and/or nightmares. ("What's pushed down must come up later.")

Some good guiding statements are:

- "It's good to talk."
- "A problem shared is a problem halved."

Up until recently, our military tradition of "stiff upper lip" and "button up" has been the way to deal with all that is seen, done and heard about in theatre. While some purposes are served by this approach in the short term, in the longer term, time and time again, it has been shown *not to be good for our health.* We need to express it, safely, in some way or another. This may be done either by the spoken word, "writing, reading and burning", or high-energy physical exercise (see later sections).

Be Careful Whom You Tell

Some people are not able to cope with what they hear, so may protect themselves by simply not believing you. Others simply will not understand. Some will glaze over as you tell them; still more, will show you no understanding or empathy while you are telling them. Many can't keep confidences and will be bursting to tell someone else what you have told them. Others will not be appropriate because of their "civvy mind". Often it is better to hand-pick an appropriate comrade or ex-comrade to "buddy-up" with: one you can trust; who understands; who can relate to what you tell him. It is not a weakness, but a sign of strength and courage to share your experiences in ways that are helpful to you, in the long run.

While it is a helpful general rule that you don't talk to civvies, many military welfare workers are either ex-servicemen; have been brought up within service environments; or have had so many years' experience within military welfare services that it is almost as good as having served, in terms of the knowledge and expertise gained.

"The okay civvy worker"

A young Guardsman, who had been involved in an ambush where comrades were lost, felt he couldn't talk to the young middle-aged female welfare worker "because she wouldn't have a clue". After being persuaded to do so by a mate who had found her helpful, he discovered that her father had been in the army and therefore she had lived on many different camps, home and abroad, each time he had been posted. Also, she had been in post for a number of years, which meant she had heard just about everything she was to hear about what could happen to service personnel.

3. "Get in Some 'De-grimming' or Black Humour"

The ability to use humour or to de-grim situations by some quip or other is a quality that enables armed forces personnel to overcome the most horrendous situations. There are countless examples of how this has been helpful in many campaigns over the past two or three centuries. Black humour has been used to good effect, both in the height of battle and afterwards. It helps us lighten an otherwise grim situation, deal with it on the spot or "put it away" more safely in our memory, until such a time when it can be dealt with more effectively.

Examples:

- A platoon commander, after a firefight, noticed a rip in the top of a young private's tin hat. He said, "You had a close shave with that round!" The private's reply was, "I think, Sir, he was trying to part my hair!"

- A Royal Marine who had lost both legs in an incident involving an IED, said joyfully, "I'm now able to compete in the Paralympics!"
- A sailor who suffered burns to his hands and forearms when one of the Royal Fleet Auxiliaries was hit in San Carlos Bay, during the Falklands War, said, "At least now, at parties, I've got a conversation starter."

4. "The Letter from the Future"[1]

This letter is to be written and not posted.

Pick a time in the future: 5, 10, 15, 20 years from now, or any number of years – longer or shorter – that is meaningful to you. Date the top of the letter with the imaginary future date. Imagine that the intervening years have passed and you are writing to a friend (pick someone you know and like in the present time). Use the friend's name: "Dear (friend's name)". Or, if you prefer, pick some other supportive person to whom you can imagine writing to, comfortably.

[1] With full acknowledgement to Milton Erickson for the original idea and to Lucia Capacchione (1979) for an earlier version.

The purpose of dating the letter, and writing it to someone you actually know, is to strengthen the psychological realism of the letter for you on both a subconscious and conscious level. Imagine that, in this future, you have resolved whatever problems are troubling you at the present time. Describe what helped you resolve those problems. At the time of the letter writing, you are living a wonderful, joyous, healthy and satisfying life. Describe how you are spending your time, where you are living, your relationships, beliefs and reflections on the past and future.

How to Use the Letter from the Future

Now that you have completed the letter, what did you learn? What did you include in the letter that is not yet happening in your life? What would be the smallest step in your actual behaviour or reactions that you could take towards making one of those things begin to happen?[2] When do you want to try that first small step?

[2]Sometimes people ask, "Why imagine the smallest step? Why not big, glorious steps?" The aim here is not to make whatever changes you desire become unintimidating, but to scale them down to a level that is comfortably achievable for you, so that your goal is reachable. It is not that people fail to make changes because they are lazy. What passes for laziness is usually fear, demoralisation or despair. The smallness of these signs is intended to overcome fear and demoralisation, and to allow you to complete your own version of the proverbial "Chinese Journey of a Thousand Miles", one small achievable step at a time. If the steps you identify seem too small, simply make them slightly larger, taking care to make them no larger than is "do-able" in the next day or two. Then proceed. Remember, if the process stalls, or if you become overwhelmed or stuck, check to see if the goal is truly what you want, and, if so, ask yourself if the step needs to be made smaller. Keep making it smaller until it is one you can do. Don't give up; you deserve the life you want.

What difference would that small step make if it continued over time? Are other small steps needed? What would be the next smallest one? What will the result(s) be for each of the steps you can identify? When do you want to start? If not, is it the wrong goal? If you want to start, but feel stuck, are there any advantages to not starting? If so, is there some way that some of the advantages of not starting (such as extra time, etc.) could be preserved to some degree without your staying stuck? What will be the consequences (how will you feel in 5, 10, 15, 20 years) if you do not start? The purpose of this question is to identify your motivation. If you still want to start, don't be discouraged by the smallness of steps. If you need inspiration for the power of small steps, go and interview a successful quilt maker, or writer, or tile layer, or anyone who does work that progresses gradually. In fact, what work doesn't progress gradually? You are your own greatest project!

5. "Changing the Mind-set"

This is a useful technique to use with a service user who has a fixed belief about a situation (e.g., Alec in "Tackle the guilt trip" earlier in this section).

Before changing the (fixed) mind-set, it is important to "loosen the negative thinking around the edges". This means sowing seeds of doubt about its validity; highlighting strengths, abilities and resources in him as a person; and, if possible, flagging up how some of these were used in the situation. Also, questions such as "What would you do more of or do differently next time, should a similar incident occur?" and "What might be the smallest, positive thing you have taken away from the incident?" may be helpful.

Once the edges of the negative thinking have been loosened sufficiently, the following types of statements can be made, as appropriate:

- "You did the best you could under the circumstances."
- "You were simply doing your job."
- "You had to think and act quickly. Sometimes in instances such as these, mistakes are made."
- "It was either you or them: what other choices did you have?"
- "Sometimes on life's journey, shocking/distressing/ frightening/upsetting things like this happen to us. In what ways has this made you a stronger person?"
- "It seems you were in the right place at the wrong time."
- "It seems you were in the right place at the right time."
- "It seems you were in the wrong place at the right time."
- "Sometimes in life, we do something terrible. However, rather than beating ourselves up about it, we can try to forgive ourselves. We may also ask for God's forgiveness."
- "With some things that happen, for which we feel responsible, we can pay back in some way by doing good for others. What might you do, if you were so inclined?"
- "You can either look at your injuries as 'the end of the world', or you can decide how you can live life to the full, despite them."

- "So what would you say you have learned as a result of this experience?"
- Add your own:
- Add your own:
- Add your own:

6. "How to Beat the 'If Only …' Monster on the Shoulder"

"If only …" can be a handicapping recurrent thought for us, in that it has the powerful result of keeping us stuck in the present.

Combat stress survivors have found this activity both highly effective and fun to do.

The technique is an adaptation of that used by Frederike Jacob (2001). Personnel are encouraged to "externalise the problem" by sitting it on their shoulder, in such a way that it can be seen as an object in its own right, rather than as an internal part of them.

Once it is sat on their shoulder, not only can they get a good look at it, in its entirety, but also they can get into direct and assertive conversation with it. The objective of these conversations is to beat it/outsmart it/defeat it/put it on the back foot, etc. Most personnel prefer "beat it" because of the triple meanings of this phrase: "successfully argue against it";

"beat it physically"; and "persuade it to beat it (leave altogether)".

"If only …", if allowed to persist, is very controlling and disempowering. The serviceman must regain both power and control. This technique achieves both.

How is it achieved? Sometimes it is helpful for the serviceman to describe his "if only …" monster, once he has taken it out of his body and placed it on his shoulder. The most important part of the technique is the next part, when he comes up with three or four things he would like to say to his monster, in order to begin defeating it. Some typical commands are:

- "It's happened, and there's nothing anyone can do about it!"
- "Shut up! Get out of my life. I'm moving on."
- "Go and take a running jump! And I hope you will kill yourself!"
- "I'll give you more than 'if only …', if you don't shut it!"

… and ruder and more explicit commands …!

As with others, it is helpful if the person practises the technique right now in the session, just after he has heard about it, and then practises it about 10–12 times a week, for a few weeks. This will make sure the power and control are transferred back from "the monster" to himself.

"I dispatched the 'if only …' monster"

A Special Forces Warrant Officer, working in a land-locked country in the southern hemisphere, had entrusted the safety of two of his sleeping comrades to two trusted natives, while he went off to set up a position. The natives fell asleep "on watch", and were killed by insurgents before they killed his comrades.

The serviceman, filled with remorse, who had been drinking and smoking heavily for many months, kept saying:

"If only I had not trusted them …"

"If only we had found a more isolated and secure position to rest up …"

"If only one of the others had argued against my decision …"

Eventually, by going through the procedure outlined, the soldier started to say the right things to the "if only …" monster; began to cut down on his drinking; and was able to move on.

7. "Write, Read and Burn (or Write, Read and Shred)"[3]

Based on a technique from the Milwaukee Brief Therapy Centre, the purpose of this exercise is to resolve any negative memories that are intruding upon and constricting the person's life in the present, in the form of flashbacks or any other kind of intrusive negative thought or image.

The person is instructed to follow these four steps:

i.   First of all, write down the details of the memory, thought, or image that troubles you.

ii. Now, write down any feelings you have about the memory, thought or image. If another person is involved in the memory, address these feelings to that person, where appropriate. Include anything you would wish to say or wish you could say to that person.

iii. Now re-read what you have written, reading it aloud.[4]

iv. Once you have done so, burn or shred the pages.

8. "Park It ...   and Move on ..."

A powerful instruction to the mind for dealing with intrusive thoughts, this technique is a simple statement that acknowledges simply that the incident occurred, without

[3] With full acknowledgement to Yvonne Dolan and Charlie Johnson for the original version. Handouts provided at training workshops.

[4] While not essential, it is sometimes helpful psychologically to have another person present (e.g., a buddy, welfare worker) to hear what you read and witness the burning or shredding of the pages.

attempting to bury it in any way. This has been of great help to personnel in both military and civilian contexts.

As a car parking metaphor, it is helpful because the serviceman can conjure up a picture of parking an old car anywhere he chooses (a lay-by, car park, roadside, etc.) – and then walking away from it – and onward, along his life journey.

He may choose to return to the car, from time to time, to take a fresh look at it; maybe sit inside for a while; or drive it around a little. In whichever case, he can park it again – lock it up – move on – and return to his walk along his life's journey.

This metaphor is powerful in another way, because what becomes of cars when they are left parked-up and neglected for a long period of time? They become dusty, covered in cobwebs, the tyres deflate, and brakes and clutch plates become seized. Eventually they become a rusty heap, fit for nothing and certainly, after many years, not something you would want to revisit anyway. By this time, a great distance has been covered between the "parked" car and the person's journey along the path of life. What happens is that, although the car is an important part of his life, its potential to affect it in the present weakens further and further. It begins to become but a distant memory.

It is helpful for the serviceman to practise saying this command: **"Park it ...   and move on"** in the session. Saying it between 10 and 12 times a week, when unwelcome thoughts occur, for a number of weeks, is about right for bedding-in this technique thoroughly.

"Parking the faces of dead enemy combatants"

A Special Forces Officer who had worked behind enemy lines in many theatres of war over a 15-year period, had a number of key intrusive thoughts that kept surfacing. Each time a particular one emerged, he would revisit it in his mind's eye (e.g., return to the "parked car"), before repeating to himself **"Park it ...   and move on"**.

9. "Let It Go ...
Let It Go ...
Let It Go ..."

This technique is very powerful for dealing with unwelcome thoughts. Rather than the serviceman trying to push down the unpleasant thought when it arises, which it is well known *does not work,* the following instruction is given:

i.   Acknowledge, briefly, the unpleasant thought.
ii. Accept that it is unwelcome and not wanted.
iii. Say to yourself, quietly but firmly: "Let it go ...   Let it go ...   Let it go ..."

10. "Fast-Forwarding the DVD of Your Life"

Fast-forwarding the DVD is used to:

• by-pass problem thinking

- create a context for setting well-formed goals
- encourage expectations of change
- get information about *how* a serviceman can make progress
- find out about things he can do, which will get him to where he wants to be.

Fast-Forwarding the DVD

Before asking the serviceman the key question of this technique, it is important to get a sufficient amount of information about their current difficulties or problem situation.

Next, it is crucial to get their full attention. This is achieved best by adopting a slight air of mystery, then asking, "Can I ask you a rather unusual question?" In my 15 years of asking this question, I have yet to have anyone decline. As human beings, we are too curious!

Once they have agreed to the question being asked, ensure you lower your tone of voice and slow down your pace of speech. This is important.

Then, when you have their full attention, ask the questions on page 91 of the workbook (Section 6).

Some people find the fast-forwarding the DVD question easier to deal with than others. It involves some creative thinking to get a clear picture of something to do that is realistic, achievable, measurable and something they want to have happen.

"I kicked into touch, both the booze and the cigs"

An ex-serviceman, who had been deployed in four theatres of operations over a seven-year career, had been medically discharged because of "alcoholism". He had received medical and drug treatment only. He was referred to an NHS community mental health team for help. The worker found him living in poverty, in a small flat that was filthy. Ashtrays piled with dog-ends, and empty wine and spirits bottles adorned most surfaces, and he was in a neglected and dishevelled state.

When asked the fast-forwarding the DVD question, he answered:

"I will have got control of all this drinking …"
"I will have sorted my life out …"
"I will have this place (looking around) tidied up …"

What else …?

"The smoking, I'll be down to no more than five a day…"
"Maybe, too, I'll have spoken to those in that Help Office, at the Regeneration Project …"

And what else …?

"I can't see myself working yet, but maybe I'll have a few ideas …"
"And … I'll have sorted my head out more, so I won't need the drink to block it out … Doesn't work for long anyway."

11. "Ways to Deal with Anger Build-Ups"

Anger is a commonly occurring feature arising from many combat experiences, and it is quite normal and understandable. But it can become a problem if we don't deal with it (i.e. get it out of the way safely, as it starts to build). First, we must recognise it. Second, we need to put in a plan of action to deal with it in a safe, healthy and controlled way.

In the following pages there are some ideas and some techniques with which to encourage service personnel to do this.

There are four main ways to deal effectively with anger.

Chat to a Military "Buddy"/Ex-comrade/Welfare Worker/Padre

"A problem shared is a problem halved" is the main principle that is working here. Telling a buddy or ex-comrade you can trust and who will keep what you say confidential, can be a great relief and a release for any anger build-up. This may be done "over a pint" or in some other setting: whatever is most helpful. Welfare workers and padres talk to thousands of combatants every year – in great confidence – and to the great benefit to combatants across all four armed services.

Write It Down

Many thousands of personnel have found it helpful to write down the emerging anger feelings and where they have arisen from. It is important for them to write as much as they need to and this can be done either on writing paper, in a journal or in a personal diary.

Service users must be encouraged to take great care to keep what they write confidential. If they use loose-leaf paper, there is the option always to burn or shred it afterwards. If a journal or personal diary is used, make sure it is kept in a safe and secure place. It is important to be careful what is committed to paper, just in case secrecy and confidentiality are compromised. Using a personal code or abbreviations can be helpful for when referring to people, places and events.

Do "Strenuous Phys"

Many, many serving personnel have found that strenuous physical exercise has a positive, discharging effect for any anger build-ups. This may involve a workout in the gym; a circuit training round; kicking a football; going for a long cycle ride; jogging; using a punchbag; or anything else that is harmless, in whatever way. With any of us, when anger builds, it is best to keep away from others until we have found our own way to discharge it safely. (Being in the presence of others, however close they are to us, can be provocative. Arguments can arise, which lead to anger spilling over in the direction of people we love and/or hold dear, in unhealthy or damaging ways.)

When encouraging servicemen to use this technique, it is helpful for them to explain to those closest to them their need to be on their own at these times, to get on with their own particular chosen workout. Once others understand this, the majority are fine with it. Some couples, especially, have a particular code word they use for this need for personal space to get on and apply the appropriate technique.

"Boxer-cise circuits"

A trooper, who had many angry feelings about some situations he had been involved in while serving in Iraq, found it really helpful to do a couple of rounds of "boxer-cise" circuits in the gym, when his anger level built. His code word to his wife at these times was "build-up". She would reply "Okay", and all would be fine once he returned from the gym.

Find Somewhere Safe to Shout!

A number of returning personnel find it very helpful to shout out, as loudly as they want or need to, about things that have caused them to feel angry in a combat situation. So as not to alarm others(!) – especially those close to them – it is important to find somewhere isolated and safe in which to have a good shout!

Some good examples of places to use are:

- in a parked car, in an isolated spot, with all windows shut firmly
- along a coastal path or on a beach
- along a footpath in between large fields in open country
- in a sound-proofed room or building.

"My so-called best mate"

A submariner, whose "best mate" had dated his partner while he had been away on exercises, was furious at both his partner and his so-called "best mate". He wanted the relationship to get back on track; and he still wanted to be friends with his mate. He knew, initially, it would be unwise and unsafe to "have it out" with each of them. So, in order to discharge the overwhelming anger safely, he parked his car in a lay-by on a rarely used country road, to shout at them, in their absence. He told the welfare worker: "I was quite hoarse when I'd finished, but I felt better!"

A few sessions later, he was able to speak to them individually, without wanting to thump either of them or any inanimate object.

12. Change Your Mental Attitude to the Unwelcome Thoughts

- It is the way we respond to unwanted thoughts that causes us distress.
- It is our reaction that enables these thoughts to have power and influence over us.
- The more we try and push unwanted thoughts away, the more they will struggle to get back into our conscious mind (e.g. see what happens when you tell yourself: "Whatever you do, *do not* think of pink elephants!").
- To hang around, thoughts need to be fed by attention, but what they love really is a good strong emotional reaction to make them stick.

Servicemen can be helped by giving them the following instruction: **A four-step approach to changing your mental attitude:**

i. Welcome the unwanted thought (or fear).
ii. Imagine a cartoon character (e.g. Tom Cat from Tom and Jerry, or Donald Duck).
iii. Give it a squeaky voice.
iv. Have the cartoon character speak out the thought (e.g. "Remember the December 2009 incident in Helmand Province?").

The result of the cartoon imagery is to re-programme the initial fearful emotional reaction – and take out the power it has over the person.

The less he fears the thought, the less likely it is to occur during the day. The emotional reaction has been neutralised.

13. Visualisation

This is done best when either sitting or standing and should last from 10 to 15 minutes. It achieves the objective of enabling the service user to regain control over anxious or unwanted thoughts, when it has been practised daily for a few weeks. When performed immediately after "let it go …   let it go …   let it go …" (see page 46), it has even more power over anxious thoughts of any type.

The mind needs to release regularly what it is holding on to. When it does, soothing and beneficial results are achieved.

With practice, this technique enables the person to release all stress within minutes of starting the exercise. They will have trained their brain. Daily practice before bedtime enables people to sleep more soundly.

Servicemen can be given the following instructions.

i. In either the sitting or the standing position, gently move your attention to your breath.

ii. Place one hand on your stomach and the other on your upper chest.

iii. Take in a breath, letting your stomach swell forward as you do so; letting it fall back on the out-breath. (Your hand on your chest should have no or little movement.)

iv. Repeat this for three times, lengthening the in-breath to the count of 7; and the out-breath to the count of 11. (This is called 7/11 diaphragmatic breathing and is described in detail in Section 1.) The more you practise 7/11 breathing, the more you will strengthen the diaphragmatic muscle and the more it will work how it is meant to.[5]

v. Now slow it down even more by adding a short pause after the out-breath, before breathing in again. (At first, you might feel you are not getting enough air but, with practice, you will become more comfortable with it.)

vi. If unwanted or intrusive thoughts come to mind as you do this, simply let them go on the out-breath, focusing back on your breathing.

---

[5] www.wisegeek.com/what-is-the-diaphragm-muscle.htm

vii. Now, move your attention to your feet, trying to really feel them. See if, one-by-one, you can feel each toe.

viii. Now visualise the soles of your feet with roots growing slowly downwards, deep into the earth beneath. Visualise the roots growing more quickly and firmly now into the earth, so that you are now rooted to the spot like a magnificent oak tree.

ix. Concentrate on this feeling of being grounded securely and safely for a minute or so.

x. Now visualise a cloud of bright light forming up high above you.

xi. Notice, now, how a bolt of lightening shoots down from the cloud on to the top of your head. As it does, it transforms itself into a circular band of white light that descends slowly down from your head, past your shoulders, waist and legs, down to your toes. As it passes downward, feel it clearing away any rubbish you may have been thinking about, so that now you have a clear and free mental state.

xii. Repeat this image of the circular band of light passing down your body about five times, until you feel a sense of all anxious thinking being cleared away and released.

xiii. Now, visualise yourself standing under a large luminescent waterfall where you are able to breathe easily.

The water is bubbling, radiant, cleansing and full of vitality.

Feel the water, washing down your body, soothing and calming you as it does so.

Hear the splash of the water on the ground all around you.

As you enjoy this experience, even more, tell yourself that not only is the water life itself, but it is washing away any anxiety, stress or worry from both your mind and your body.

xiv. After a few moments, and in your own time, open your eyes. Then, gently and slowly move away to what you were doing before, or want to do next. (Avoid ripping too much of the ground away, as your tree roots are severed!)

This visualisation, like many others, achieves the twin objectives of restoring calm and replacing a sense of lack of control with one of *control.*

14. The Solution-focused Feelings Tank

Sometimes an unwanted thought is connected to a negative feeling we have about a situation. This negative feeling can be any one or several of the following:

Anger	Hurt
Disappointment	Being overwhelmed
Fear	Rage
Guilt	Regret
Sadness	Worry
Shame	Helplessness

Because these negative feelings can, if we let them, take control of us, it is important to take the control back. How do we do this? One very effective way is to use the "solution-focused feelings tank".

First, it is important for the worker to explain to the serviceman how the tank may be used. It is a garden water butt, containing whatever quantity of the particular negative feeling they may have right now (e.g. anger, disappointment, regret).

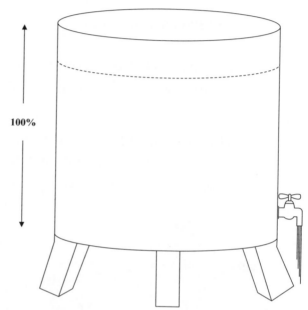

Figure 3.1   The solution-focused feelings tank

The explanation then goes as follows:

i.   "There is no inlet pipe, but there is a tap, over which you have control."
ii. "You will never empty the feelings tank about this situation (i.e. anger in this case), because the tap is at a higher level than the bottom of the tank."
iii. "How much anger have you managed to run off through this tap, so far?"

Suppose they say "3%"?

iv. "Three per cent! How have you managed to do *that*?"

Service user answers ...

iv. "What's the next small step you could take to run off another 1% over the next two to three weeks?"

Service user answers …

v. "And what else could you do, to get the level down by just another 1%?" … and so on.

This exercise has proved to be very helpful in empowering clients to take control of whatever negative feeling keeps popping up in the form of an unwanted thought. It is also a very affirming exercise, because only occasionally will someone answer that their tank if 100% full. The majority of clients answer 70–95%. So, some credit can be given for what actions or changes in thinking have taken place already.

Section 4
Dealing with "The Lows"

1. Work at, and maintain, a good balanced diet
2. Drink plenty of liquids
3. Remind yourself of the power of humour
4. Do something pleasurable for the sake of it
5. Build up your physical fitness or a sufficient level of physical activity
6. Keep self-confidence and self-esteem at a high level
7. See "the lows" as a virus that can be dealt with
8. Get out there and get reconnected with supportive people
9. Acknowledge to yourself that you have a touch of "the lows"
10. Increase your knowledge/get more information
11. Get enough sleep
12. "The Rainy Day Letter"
13. "Don't just lie there, get up!"
14. Breathe your way to a relaxed state
15. If you let "the lows" get too low

One thing is for certain, and that is that all service personnel we see will have low days as they make their journey back to full recovery and control. The good news is that, as they

Beating Combat Stress: 101 Techniques for Recovery. By John Henden.
© 2011 John Wiley & Sons Ltd.

master the tools and techniques in this handbook, they will be more in control, more often. This means they will not be controlled by negative thinking and the "lows" that accompany them. However, it is not realistic to think we can prevent all low days. There will be times when servicemen feel they are not getting anywhere, and are asking questions such as "What is it all about anyway?", "I feel just like giving up", etc. We need to help them with having a plan or strategy ready for when these days happen.

1. Work at, and Maintain, a Good Balanced Diet

As we are resolving reactions to past events, there can be a tendency to "comfort eat".

This does us no favours at all. Nor does it do any favours to our family and friends, who have to cope with our reduced agility, poorer health and lower energy levels. The trouble is, "comfort eating" tends to consist mainly of all the wrong things: chocolate, sweets, biscuits, fast food, and fizzy drinks.

Contrary to some opinions, healthy eating need not be expensive. Often, in fact, it can be cheaper. Ensure you get your "five-a-day" fruit and vegetables. A healthy intake of the whole range of vitamins and minerals all help toward feeling good. Cut down on saturated fat, salt and sugar, too.

2. Drink Plenty of Liquids

Ensuring that you drink 2–3 litres of liquids, in various forms, every day, will mean both that you feel better and that your brain and body function as they should. Headaches, too, can be avoided. A car engine running on little oil will not perform as well as if there is a good measured level on the dipstick. Drinking water is preferable, but fruit juice, squash or hot beverages are okay too. With the latter two, care needs to be taken about not taking in too much sugar and caffeine, neither of which are healthy.

3. Remind Yourself of the Power of Humour

Usually, a good sign that we are feeling low is that our sense of humour goes. Answer: Get it going again! Do this by watching a comic DVD, internet searching for humorous websites or reading a joke book.

Laughter is a good antidote to feeling low. There is plenty of evidence to prove that chemicals released into the bloodstream by laughter help us to feel better.

4. Do Something Pleasurable for the Sake of It

Everyone has their preferred way(s) of deriving personal pleasure or satisfaction. If space allowed, I could list over 1000! Although you might not feel up to doing it right now, you will feel the benefit of doing something pleasurable anyway.

5. Build up Your Physical Fitness or a Sufficient Level of Physical Activity

Fit body means fit mind. Everyone can do something to improve their level of physical fitness or physical activity. It is a good daily discipline to get into.

It can range from a full boxer-cise workout in the gym to gentle arm swinging and arm and waist tensioning from a chair – and all points in between.

Again, a lot of scientific evidence is available to prove how we feel better when we get involved in some form of exercise, whether "high-burn" or gentle.

6. Keep Self-confidence and Self-esteem at a High Level

Self-confidence and self-esteem are inter-connected. If we have feelings that we have little personal value, our confidence is low too. If we feel low in confidence, we will not value ourselves very much either.

The answer is to tackle either one or the other, to boost up both.

"I *live* in this village"

An injured veteran had been both withdrawn and isolated from others in his village for many months. He lacked the confidence to go out, having a whole collection of helpers who would bring things to him. Walking was painful because of the extent of injuries received in theatre. Also, he had a slight limp. In addition to his low self-confidence, his self-esteem was low too: he felt worthless, believing he had nothing to contribute to anyone.

With the help of a veterans' welfare worker, he was able to tell himself:

> "I have every right to walk around the village; I have served my country well and can hold my head up high; and going for a short walk in the evening, first, will build up my confidence for a longer walk tomorrow."

Result: Eventually he walked into the village most days; he got to know other villagers better; he was invited to play in a local skittles team; he built up his social life; he spent two days a week in voluntary work; and he was thinking of meeting up with a local job centre advisor regarding future paid employment opportunities.

7. See "The Lows" as a Virus That Can Be Dealt with

"The lows" virus finds good breeding ground if our confidence and self-esteem are low; we are feeling "stressed-out"; we are run down physically; we are holding in our thoughts and feelings; and we are feeling full of anger and resentment. *Anyone* can find themselves in this situation, at some point in their life.

The important thing to do to defend against or defeat this virus is to work hard at all the items in this section. Once achieved, the results will be:

- clearer thinking
- improved sense of humour
- higher self-confidence and self-esteem
- better mood
- higher energy levels.

8. Get Out There and Get Reconnected with Supportive People

Withdrawal and isolation are common results of "the lows". Even though it may seem very hard or near-impossible, it is vital to get reconnected. Old comrades; the regimental association; a supportive buddy; friendly neighbours – anyone supportive, who you can talk to in confidence.

The principle that operates is: "A problem shared is a problem halved!" Tell yourself it is okay to talk about thoughts and feelings with people you trust, even though you might have been told sometime ago that this was not permitted. Once you've done this, notice the difference made to how you feel about yourself.

9. Acknowledge to Yourself That You Have a Touch of "The Lows"

... then take action.

Often, *anything* we do can get us back to feeling okay again. The domino effect applies. It doesn't matter what we

do: giving ourselves a good talking to; taking some
physical action; writing out thoughts, ideas and feelings
on the situation; or talking to someone we trust:
all can start the domino process going.

10. Increase Your Knowledge/Get More Information

Searching the internet; reading booklets or pamphlets;
discussing with a welfare worker can all help
increase our knowledge about "the lows" and how to
tackle them. People used to feel they were going
mad or "losing it" in some way before they got to know
that it is a normal, understandable situation to get into
when we don't take good enough care of ourselves.

11. Get Enough Sleep

It is not quantity of sleep that is important,
but *quality*. When unresolved thoughts go
round and round in our minds, it is hard to
get into deep sleep. It may be difficult to get
off to sleep; get back to sleep on waking in the night; or stop
waking very early. Sometimes, even though we might have
slept for nine hours, if it has not been of sufficient
quality (deep sleep), we may wake tired and feeling
exhausted.

(For many, many tips and ideas for improving sleep, go to
Section 5.)

12. "The Rainy Day Letter"[1]

While some of life's difficult passages are impossible to anticipate, thankfully they are not impossible to prepare for; that is the purpose of **The "Rainy Day Letter"**. It can function as a bridge over life's chasms, not in the sense of providing numbing or "faking" the experience, but rather as a way to help transform difficult moments into experiences of mastery and hope. It is ironic that the very times when we need to remember strengths and resources most, are often those occasions when it is easiest to forget about them. **The "Rainy Day Letter"** or, if you prefer, **"Rainy Day Postcards"** are a way to remind one of strengths and resources at those very times, when they are most needed.

The instructions to give the person are as follows:

How to Make Your Own "Rainy Day Letter"

This is a letter from you to you. It should be written not in a moment of despair, but in a moment of relative calm and well-being. It is an emotional insurance policy against the inevitability of those darker moments that come at various times in life, a sort of 'emergency road-side repair kit' for the spirit. The letter should contain, but is not limited to, the following:

- A list of nurturing activities to do.
- A list of nurturing people to call.

[1] Yvonne Dolan, M.A. and Charlie Johnson, M.S.W. Copyright 1995; excerpted from Dolan (2000).

- Reminders of your positive character traits.
- Reminders of spiritual or philosophical beliefs that strengthen you.
- Reminders of some of your dreams and hopes for the future.
- Special advice or other reminders important to you.

Once completed, put the "Rainy Day Letter" in a place where you can easily find it whenever needed. Some people like to make several copies so that they can carry one in a wallet, briefcase or purse, leave one in a special drawer or car glove compartment, etc.

13. "Don't Just Lie There, Get Up!"

When we wake up in the morning and just continue lying there, the mind goes into overtime: it starts to work on the issues and concerns in our lives. These issues and concerns then seem 10 times worse than when we are up and about.

Keeping it simple, a chemical process starts in the brain and the body, releasing bad chemicals into our system. These start flowing through our arteries, with unpleasant results.

It is important, in cases where an ex-serviceman has fallen into this habit, to get them to experiment, so as to notice the difference and benefits when they get up and get going, rather than just lying there.

14. Breathe Your Way to a Relaxed State

Find somewhere comfortable to sit or lie. Then, with your eyes lightly closed, empty your mind of all current thoughts. Now, after a short, slow breath in, breathe out slowly and steadily for the count of 11. Hold it for about two seconds. Then, breathe in again for the count of 7. Repeat this about six or seven times. The more controlled and deliberate you are, the deeper will be your sense of relaxation. To maintain the effects for a good while after, wait a few minutes, before slowly and carefully getting up and moving on to another activity. (This technique is described in detail in Section 1.)

15. If You Let "The Lows" Get Too Low

Sometimes, while going through a period of "the lows", we can let a situation spiral downwards. This is unpleasant, to say the least, as those of us who have been there can testify. Should this happen, call a "Halt!" immediately, promising yourself that you will take the first small step back – *and* within the next hour.

Should you be feeling so low that suicidal thoughts and ideas enter your mind, then there are plenty of options to take. One of these is to read through the many tools and techniques in my book about preventing suicidal thoughts (Henden, 2008). Another is to speak to a welfare worker, the padre or your medical officer. The Samaritans is an option, too.

Remember, suicide is a permanent solution to a short-term problem, and should be seen as such!

Section 5
Dealing with Sleep Disturbance

A. Techniques for Preparing for Bed

1. Read a book
2. Have some cereal or a milky drink
3. Watch a happy or boring film
4. Establish a soothing routine
5. Get enough exercise
6. Eat early
7. Prepare well for bedtime
8. Open the window a little
9. Use lavender oil
10. Listen to a story
11. Complete some tasks
12. Turn off the late news
13. Sort out your curtains
14. Resolve disagreements
15. Go for mattress comfort
16. Alternate quilts with the seasons
17. Go for softer pillows
18. Drink relaxing teas
19. Put your worries on hold
20. Buy some earplugs
21. Steer clear of caffeine and chocolate

Beating Combat Stress: 101 Techniques for Recovery. By John Henden.
© 2011 John Wiley & Sons Ltd.

22. Undress slowly for bed
23. "Larks" and "owls" help each other
24. Reduce emotional and psychological stress

B. Getting off to Sleep

1. Lie flat and stare
2. Count sheep
3. Use "reverse psychology"
4. Turn your pillow
5. Tense and then relax your muscles
6. Count backwards
7. Read through the whole of this sub-section
8. Listen through headphones
9. Go for absolute stillness
10. Relax your shoulders
11. Worry not
12. Visualise calm scenes
13. Practise 7/11 breathing
14. Relax your jaws

C. Getting Back to Sleep, If Waking or Awakened in the Night

1. Think relaxing words
2. Make a list of worrying thoughts
3. Use your favourite guided fantasy
4. Tell yourself sleep doesn't matter
5. Watch some TV
6. Get up and read

7. Pray for people
8. Forgive right now
9. Turn your quilt
10. Get up and do it right now
11. Crawl into a "safe and secure tunnel"
12. Use the 5-4-3-2-1 method

It is important for us to talk through, or in some way resolve, traumatic or disturbing memories and thoughts during the hours we are awake. If we do not do this, or we try and suppress them with drugs or alcohol, our brain will get stuck into these memories and thoughts overnight, while we are asleep. This can be the stuff of nightmares. Often, we are awakened by this activity and don't find it easy getting back to sleep. The main purpose of dreaming is to resolve the unresolved conflicts of the day. Better, then, to try and resolve as many conflicts as we can during our waking hours. That is what Sections 1–4 have been about.

 Prevention is better than cure. It is better if we sort out conflicts and painful memories by using the tools and techniques outlined in those earlier sections. However, in the following pages are some tips for preparing for bed; getting off to sleep; and getting back to sleep if we have been awakened by a disturbing dream.

The following tips are addressed directly to servicemen who have experienced COSR but anyone can try them out for effectiveness. When workers or practitioners try out these tips for themselves, then they are then more likely to recommend them.

A. Techniques for Preparing for Bed

It is helpful to create a "no-man's land" between day and night. This can be done by preparing for bedtime at least half an hour before getting into bed.

1. Read a Book

A good way to empty our minds of all the cares and concerns of the day is to read an easygoing book, last thing at night.

2. Have Some Cereal or a Milky Drink

Many have found that a bowl of cereal or a milky drink before going to bed is helpful. This diverts blood from the thinking brain to the stomach, to help digestion.

3. Watch a Happy or Boring Film

The activity of watching a happy or boring film or DVD before going to bed puts a line under the day's cares and helps you prepare for sleep. Some TV programmes can have the same effect.

4. Establish a Soothing Routine

Within half an hour to one hour before going to bed, use a soothing routine that suits you best. This might involve having a soak in a hot bath, listening to your favourite music, etc.

5. Get Enough Exercise

Make sure each day is well balanced with adequate mental and physical exercise. Gentle exercise taken an hour or so after your evening meal promotes relaxation and aids digestion.

6. Eat Early

Eat your evening meal at least one and a half to two hours before bedtime. This avoids the "heaviness" that can be felt after a large meal, when trying to go off to sleep. With technique 2 on page 72 in mind, it is a matter of degree.

7. Prepare Well for Bedtime

Avoid exciting, dynamic or focused activities during the late evening. Also avoid tense discussions or phone calls.

8. Open the Window a Little

Opening your bedroom window a little, so as to maintain a fresh air supply through the night, can prevent "stuffiness", thereby reducing the risk of night-time waking. A room temperature that is not too hot and not too cold will aid deep sleep.

9. Use Lavender Oil

Drops of lavender oil on your pillow can help you relax, prior to drifting off to sleep.

10. Listen to a Story

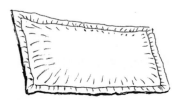

Getting immersed in a bedtime radio story is a good way of preparing for sleep.

11. Complete Some Tasks

Think of some tasks during the day that, if you made a start or completed them, would help you sleep that night (e.g., tax form, application form, loose shelving bracket, tacking down some loose carpet, etc.)

12. Turn off the Late News

As TV and radio news selected for listeners tends, in the main, to be bad news, this can affect both sleep and dreams. You are better off listening to it earlier in the day. Listening to, as opposed to watching the news, is less likely to disturb sleep.

13. Sort out Your Curtains

Buy some heavier curtains, or have some existing ones lined. Make sure all gaps are covered, so as to prevent chinks of early morning light shining through. This is especially important during the summer months.

14. Resolve Disagreements

It is helpful, where possible, to sort out any daytime disagreements you might have had with family members or friends before going to bed. Resolved disagreements are good for settled sleep.

15. Go for Mattress Comfort

It is helpful to ensure your bed is the most comfortable for you. A good mattress is not necessarily the most expensive. It is important to pay attention to this, because we spend a quarter to a third of our lives in bed. A quick-fix or cheaper option is to lay an old quilt or piece of foam under the bottom sheet.

16. Alternate Quilts with the Seasons

If using a quilt, it is important to make sure the tog rating is right for you. If finances permit, alternate with summer and winter quilts to maintain good night-time body temperatures.

17. Go for Softer Pillows

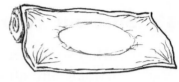

Changing your pillows for softer or
more comfortable ones can be
pleasant for both your face and head.
Experiment with two thin pillows or one thicker one.

18. Drink Relaxing Teas

Have a cup of herbal tea, such as camomile,
lemon verbena, lemon balm or peppermint
before going to bed. Alternatively, sipping
warm water can have a similar effect.

19. Put Your Worries on Hold

Before going to bed, write down your
worries, troubles or mental conflicts in a
notebook, or on a notepad, for action the next
day or at a future date.

20. Buy Some Earplugs

Fitting a suitable pair of earplugs can screen out all
but the loudest noises that might awaken you during
your time asleep. They are especially useful for light
sleepers. It is important to find the right type to suit you,
because some are more comfortable than others. This is
important if you live near a busy road, railway or under an
airport flight path. Two of the most popular types are the

condensed, shaped foam and the wax barrel-shaped. Many people prefer to cut the latter type in half before moulding them to fit. Surprisingly, while even the most effective earplugs screen out most noise (fortunately!), they do not seem to be effective against smoke alarms, fire alarms and alarm clocks.

21. Steer Clear of Caffeine and Chocolate

The stimulants within strong tea and coffee, and in chocolate, are likely to delay your getting off to sleep. Keeping them out of your diet for at least five hours before bedtime will be helpful.

22. Undress Slowly for Bed

Taking your time – plenty of time – to remove each item of clothing before sliding into bed can help the body cool down better for sleeping.

23. "Larks" and "Owls" Help Each Other

If you are a "lark", and your spouse is an "owl", it is most likely you will be first to bed on nearly all occasions. A polite request for your "owl" to enter the bedroom and get into bed quietly when they do so will reduce the risk of your being woken up. On the other hand, if you are an "owl", ask your "lark" to climb out of bed slowly and quietly, when they wake, so as not to wake you.

24. Reduce Emotional and Psychological Stress

Avoid putting yourself under too much pressure. If you do so, you will find that your stress levels stay within acceptable levels and, as a result, you are likely to sleep better. You may need to say "No" more often.

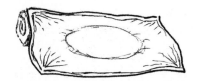

B. Getting off to Sleep

1. Lie Flat and Stare

Lie flat on your back and stare at a spot on the ceiling. Try and keep your eyelids open and still, avoiding blinking, for as long as possible.
Although it does not matter if you do blink from time to time, continue staring at your chosen point on the ceiling.

2. Count Sheep

This is probably the most well known technique. It works best when you concentrate hard on the activity, taking it seriously. Count your sheep, both on a hillside and out across the meadow and wherever else you can see them: "Two by the gate, one by the round bush", "Three by the stream", etc.

3. Use "Reverse Psychology"

Try and stay awake for as long as you can. Be as sincere and determined as possible with this. It helps if you tell yourself it doesn't matter if you don't sleep: you are resting anyway by lying flat. Many people find they are asleep sooner, rather than later, by this method.

4. Turn Your Pillow

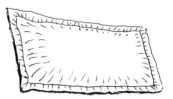

If your head is too warm, caused by too much thinking, turn the pillow over to the "cold side".

5. Tense and Then Relax Your Muscles

Beginning with your jaws, gently tense the muscles and relax them before going down through the body, right to the feet. You will feel a slight heaviness, calmness and sense of relaxation, as a result. This promotes deep sleep.

6. Count Backwards

Very slowly, count backwards in your head, in threes, from 300 down to 0.

7. Read Through the Whole of This Sub-section

If you are having difficulty sleeping, there is no better read. Choose which part you want to make use of tonight.

8. Listen Through Headphones

The act of listening softly to the radio or music, through headphones, creates a barrier between you and all that is "outside". As you feel sleepy, simply slide off the headphones and press the "off" switch on your radio, MP3 player or iPod.

9. Go for Absolute Stillness

Lie on your back very, very still, without moving a muscle. Gently resist any temptation to move. Through the stillness, sleepiness can take over.

10. Relax Your Shoulders

Consciously lowering your shoulders away from your ear-lobes can help remove the tensions of the day. First, lower the shoulders; let them return to a comfortable position; then lower them again. Let them return, before lowering them again.

11. Worry Not

When worries about the future come to mind, tell yourself you will deal with them in the coming weeks and days. Also, they often revolve around things that will **never** happen.

12. Visualise Calm Scenes

When we visualise some of our favourite calm scenes, examining each carefully in detail, this distracts from the cares of the day and helps us to relax.

13. Practise 7/11 Breathing (See Also Section 1)

This is a powerful technique for regaining control of both our body and mind. Simply breathe out for the count of 11, ensuring your abdomen contracts as you do so. Then, when all the breath is exhaled, allow your diaphragm to pull down, as you breath in slowly, for the count of 7. When done correctly, *the abdomen extends and the chest remains still.* This is important and may require practice to get it right. The result will be calmness and a greater sense of being in control of both body and mind.

14. Relax Your Jaws

By focusing on your jaw muscles, relaxing them and allowing your mouth to hang open, is a good way of reducing tension. Simply continue the 7/11 technique, breathing in through the nose and out through the mouth.

C: Getting Back to Sleep, If Waking or Awakened in the Night

1. Think Relaxing Words

Say to yourself slowly and quietly in your own mind, the following words:

"Calmness …   ", "Sleepiness …   ",
"Drowsiness …   ", "Relaxation …   ",
"Heaviness …   ", "Tranquillity …   ",
"Serenity …   ", "Peace …   ",
"Sweet dreams …   ", etc. Then, say them even more
slowly and repeat them over again for as long as necessary.

2. Make a List of Worrying Thoughts

Sometimes, worries, regrets and unresolved conflicts of the
day can awaken us in the form of vivid dreams or nightmares.
This is a natural process, although when it happens it is
unpleasant. Without turning on the light, it is helpful to list
them on a piece of paper or notepad at your bedside as soon as
you realise what has woken you up. It is important to promise
you will act on them tomorrow, towards resolving them in
some way or other. The process of writing them down like this
seems to satisfy the brain, which then allows sleep.

3. Use Your Favourite Guided Fantasy

Transport yourself to your favourite place (hillside, meadow,
beach, far off island, etc.) Call to mind five things there you
can see; five things you can hear; five things you can smell;
five things you can taste; and five things you can touch. Really
concentrate on your favourite place, experiencing sensations
such as calmness, pleasure, delight, wonder
and relaxation. Stay at your favourite place
for as long as you like, before drifting off to
sleep. Over 90% of people who use this
method say they can never remember getting
beyond halfway before sleep takes over!

4. Tell Yourself Sleep Doesn't Matter

By saying to yourself, "I don't mind if I sleep, lie awake, or gently doze. I am getting valuable rest, either way." This can take the pressure off and thereby help you to get back to sleep.

5. Watch Some TV

Get up to go and watch some trivia or something boring on night-time TV, preferably wearing a minimum of clothing. Return to bed when either you are bored or have become too cold.

6. Get up and Read

On waking in the night, get out and read an "easy-to-read" book for a chapter or few pages, before returning to bed. If you are alone in the bedroom, maybe simply sit up in bed to read.

7. Pray for People

Praying systematically for each member of your family and for your friends is both purposeful and helps distract you as you concentrate on the needs and worries of others.

8. Forgive Right Now

If you are holding a grudge or some ill-feeling towards someone, forgive them totally and unconditionally right now.

This is important because the only person being damaged by such feelings, if you allow them to persist, is *you*.

9. Turn Your Quilt

By slowly and carefully turning your quilt over to the cold side, you may cool your body down sufficiently to encourage sleep. (Best for when sleeping alone, because it could become somewhat alarming to your partner!) Another way is to peel back the covers, temporarily, and getting cool for a short while.

10. Get up and do It Right Now

If something you need to do is going round and round in your head, if practicable, get up and do it now. Then return to bed, comforting yourself in the knowledge that it's now done and out of the way.

11. Crawl into a "Safe and Secure Tunnel"

"Now, imagine you have hollowed out a small, dry, tunnel in a hillside. You have furnished it with a narrow mattress, sleeping bag and pillow. You have a small nightlight burning safely in the corner. You have carved out small shelves in the soft rock for little personal objects. Now, experience the security you feel and notice all you can see in your safe, cosy environment, before gently drifting off to sleep."

12. Use the 5-4-3-2-1 Method

This technique, which is very powerful for dealing with triggers, can also be used for getting back to sleep. Please refer to page 6 in Section 1.

Section 6

Living Life to the Full (or as Full as Possible)

This section may be photocopied and used as a personal workbook.

1. Remind yourself about your strengths, qualities, skills, resources and other personal characteristics
2. How have you used these qualities, strengths, skills, etc. up to now?
3. How will these qualities, strengths, skills, etc. be helpful to you in the future?
4. "Fast-forwarding the DVD of your life"
5. Scaling progress on the DVD of your life, as described on the TV monitor
6. What have I done or thought about that has been found to be helpful so far?
7. What has been found helpful in what others have said or done?
8. The power of small steps
9. Who are my main encouragers and/or supporters?
10. Write down dreams for the future
11. Those who have "done it", whom I most admire
12. What gives my life meaning and purpose?
13. Keeping all drugs at bay
14. Seek out intimacy in relationships

Beating Combat Stress: 101 Techniques for Recovery. By John Henden.
© 2011 John Wiley & Sons Ltd.

15. Reconnect with yourself
16. Reconnect to a community
17. Connect to God or a "higher power"
18. Write a letter to someone you really admire
19. Kick the "PTSD" label into touch
20. The amazing effect of the first small step
21. Don't buy into the "depression" label

If you are serving, or an ex-combatant, and you have had some sort of operational stress reaction (which is normal), it is not good enough simply to know you have survived whatever incident or incidents you have experienced, or were involved in. Survival alone is not living, but a form of coping or existence at a lower level. You deserve more.

Living life to the full, being as fulfilled as possible with a maximum sense of purpose must be the aim of us all. Without meaning and direction, we are simply "as straws in the wind". "Going with the flow" (or similar) is not an option. Remember, only *dead* fish go with the flow.

Within this section, you will find some tips and techniques to help you live life to the full. Yvonne Dolan (2000) outlined three stages of survival. It is the third stage (the authentic life/living life to the full/thriving) that we can all benefit by steering towards.

It may be that you have lost a limb (or limbs); have some degree of reduced physical functioning; or have some reduced brain capacity, owing to a head injury of some sort. Hearing or sight may have been affected. While acknowledging fully these limitations, it is of the greatest importance to live life as fully as possible. We owe it to ourselves and those closest to us. In fact, history is peppered with stories of people who have found that their limitations were not as limiting as they had first thought.

We know from experience that many who have been in life-threatening situations, or places of extreme danger, are thankful on their return. Most are up for a discussion under this section. There follows some tips, tools and techniques for you for opening up this discussion about living life to the full.

1. Remind Yourself about Your Strengths, Qualities, Skills, Resources and Other Personal Characteristics.

Now complete the following list:

i.   vii.

ii.   viii.

iii.   ix.

iv.   x.

v.   xi.

vi.   xii.

In addition, if your best mate was sat opposite you, what would they say, to add to the list?

i.   iv.

ii.   v.

iii.   vi.

2. How Have You Used These Qualities, Strengths, Skills, etc. up to Now?

Write down some examples of how, or in what ways, you have put some of these into practice, to get to where you are today:

a.

b.

c.

Beating Combat Stress: 101 Techniques for Recovery. By John Henden.
© 2011 John Wiley & Sons Ltd.

3. How will These Qualities, Strengths, Skills, etc. be Helpful to You in the Future?

If you are meeting up with a welfare worker or counsellor, often a good between-session task is to do the following, before the next time you see them:

With your same lists of answers to question 1, write down how some of these will be helpful as you face the challenges, decisions etc. in the future:

a.

b.

c.

d.

4. "Fast-forwarding the DVD of Your Life" (This Technique Is also Included in Section 3)

Fast-forwarding the DVD is used to:

- by-pass problem thinking
- create a context for setting well-formed goals
- encourage expectations of change
- get information about *how* you can make progress
- find out about things you can do, which will get you to where you want to be.

Fast-Forwarding the DVD

A useful question to ask yourself, is as follows below. Before doing so, make sure you have found a quiet, private place, where you will not be interrupted for about half an hour. Have a sheet of A4 paper ready for your answers.

The question:

"Just suppose, over there in the corner, there is a TV and DVD player …   In it, there is a DVD of your life in, say, six months' time, when you have got everything sorted …   In your hand there is a remote control (it is more powerful an exercise if you hold an actual remote control). You start the DVD …   What will be the first thing you will see on the TV monitor, to let you know that your problem or difficulty is now solved, or you are coping much better with any physical limitation you might have?"

… What else will you see?   … What else?

… What will you be doing differently?   … What else will you be doing?

… What different reactions might you see in those closest to you?

… What else?

… How will your thinking have changed?   … How else?

Some people find the fast-forwarding the DVD question easier to use than others. It involves some creative thinking to get a clear picture of something to do that is realistic, achievable, measurable and something you want to have happen. Be patient and persistent when doing this exercise, to gain maximum benefit.

5. Scaling Progress on the DVD of Your Life, as Described on the TV Monitor

Before scaling progress, it is helpful to make the following "link statement": "I'm wondering whether a little piece of what I have just described on the TV monitor is happening already." Write this down.

Then ask yourself:

Q: "On a scale of 1–10, where 10 stands for everything I have described on the DVD happening as fully as possible, and 1 stands for it not having started, where am I right now on this 1–10 scale?"
A: (A majority of people answer 2–4½.)
Q: "How come I am at this number and not half a point lower?"
A:
Q: "What would I need to do to move half or one full point further along, over, say, the next two to three weeks?"
A:
Q: "What will be good enough on this 1–10 scale for me?" (Most people don't need to go for perfection – at 10.)
A:

6. What Have I Done or Thought about That Has Been Found to be Helpful So Far?

With any traumatic event or extreme situation in life, not only have we survived them, we have done things that have helped us. Sometimes, we either forget or downplay these useful things we have done. It is helpful to remind ourselves – and often – just what we have done.

Write down at least three things that you have done or thought about and found to be helpful to you:

i.

ii.

iii.

iv.

v.

Beating Combat Stress: 101 Techniques for Recovery. By John Henden.
© 2011 John Wiley & Sons Ltd.

7. What Has Been Found Helpful in What Others Have Said or Done?

Some people, although they mean well, are of little help. Others, whether they be professionals, comrades or ex-comrades, friends, family, etc., are found to be helpful by things they do or say.

List a few here:

a. Person's name:
Helpful thing done or said:

b. Person's name:
Helpful thing done or said:

c. Person's name:
Helpful thing done or said:

d. Person's name:
Helpful thing done or said:

Beating Combat Stress: 101 Techniques for Recovery. By John Henden.
© 2011 John Wiley & Sons Ltd.

8. The Power of Small Steps

Sometimes we can feel overwhelmed by what lies ahead, and, as a result, not do anything towards overcoming any obstacles that might be in the way. As mentioned earlier, there is an old Chinese saying: "A journey of a thousand miles begins with the first small step." What is your first small step? Can you think of one that is an *even smaller* step, for you personally – one that can be taken within the next five to ten days?

Again, this is a useful between-session task to set yourself:

My First Small Step is:

Now, complete the following:

How and When I will Take This Small Step:

Beating Combat Stress: 101 Techniques for Recovery. By John Henden.
© 2011 John Wiley & Sons Ltd.

9. Who are My Main Encouragers and/or Supporters?

It is important to bring to mind who your main supporters and/or encouragers are. What is even more important is to write down their names and telephone numbers, and in what ways they encourage, support or nurture you. On low days, it is too easy to forget who they are and not ring or contact them. Writing down their details will help you stay connected.

a. Name: **Mobile no:**
                                      Tel. no:
                                      Email:
How they encourage/support/nurture:

b. Name: **Mobile no:**
                                        Tel. no:
                                      Email:
How they encourage/support/nurture:

c. Name: **Mobile no:**
                                        Tel. no:
                                      Email:
How they encourage/support/nurture:

d. Name: **Mobile no:**
                                        Tel. no:
                                      Email:
How they encourage/support/nurture:

Beating Combat Stress: 101 Techniques for Recovery. By John Henden.
© 2011 John Wiley & Sons Ltd.

10. Write down Dreams for the Future

With the future in mind, answer the following question with something that is both realistic, achievable, measurable and possible:

"What I would really like to do or achieve within the next few months/years/etc. is to ..."

(The importance of both visualising and writing out our dreams for the future is that we are more likely to achieve them; or, at least, move forward a few small steps in their direction.)

Beating Combat Stress: 101 Techniques for Recovery. By John Henden.
© 2011 John Wiley & Sons Ltd.

11. Those Who Have "Done It", Whom I Most Admire

Despite physical and/or psychological obstacles, many survivors of all sorts of things in life go on to live full and fulfilling lives. Reading the autobiographies of these individuals can be helpful. It may be, simply, that bringing them to mind, especially what they have managed to achieve and continue to achieve, has a similar effect on you.

Some of the more noteworthy in our current age are:

a) Simon Weston,[1] Welsh Guardsman, who received 46% burns when the Royal Fleet Auxiliary ship HMS Sir Galahad was hit by an enemy missile in San Carlos Bay, during the Falklands War in 1982.

Simon had years of reconstructive surgery, with 70 major operations or surgical procedures.

He tells his story in order to motivate and encourage those, like him, who want to move on to the next goal, whatever it

[1] www.simonweston.com

may be. His message is one of single-minded determination, not only to accept what is, but to turn that to advantage. His career demonstrates clearly how a positive mental attitude can achieve great goals.

A key saying of Simon's that has encouraged many is: "The only obstacles to achieving one's targets and successes are those you create for yourself."

Achievements:

i.   wrote a best-selling autobiography
ii. in 2005, was awarded The Most Excellent Order of The British Empire (OBE)
iii. campaigned successfully in support of troops and veterans against the alleged failures of some politicians to support them adequately.

b. Frank Gardner,[2] the BBC's Security Correspondent, who was a former Territorial Army Officer in the Royal Green Jackets. In 1998, he became the BBC's full-time Gulf correspondent, specialising in covering stories on the so-called "war on terror". In June 2004, while reporting

[2] www.wikipedia.org/wiki/Frank_Gardner

from a suburb of Riyadh, Saudi Arabia, he was shot six times and seriously injured in an attack by al Qaeda sympathisers. His cameraman colleague, Simon Cumbers, was shot dead. Being partly paralysed in his legs, Frank is now dependent on a wheelchair for life.

Achievements:

i. presented an archive-hour programme on the naturalist, Sir Peter Scott

ii. was named "Person of the Year" in 2005 by the UK Press Gazette

iii. also in 2005, was awarded an OBE for his services to journalism.

c. Phil Packer,[3] who sustained a spinal cord injury in February 2008, while serving in Iraq. After a time of rehabilitation, both in hospital and at Headley Court Rehabilitation Centre, he decided to embark upon numerous physical challenges to raise funds for charities.

In 2009, he was voted "Fundraiser of the Year". His three challenges that year were to:

[3] www.philpacker.com

  i.   walk the London Marathon within 14 days
  ii. row the English Channel with Al Humphreys
  iii. haul himself up Al Capitan (a mountain), with a support team of some of the country's best climbers.

Phil has now embarked on a new life of dedicating his time and energy to supporting young people and young people with disabilities (aged 16–25 years). He continues to inspire millions.

Other achievements:

  i.   raised over £1million for the charity "Help for Heroes"
  ii. in June 2010, was awarded an OBE.

Write down here the people who have inspired you (they don't have to be famous):

a. Name:
Achievements:

b. Name:
Achievements:

c. Name:
Achievements:

Beating Combat Stress: 101 Techniques for Recovery. By John Henden.
© 2011 John Wiley & Sons Ltd.

12. What Gives My Life Meaning and Purpose?

"If we aim for nothing, we can be fairly certain we will hit it."

This statement is as true for returnees from deployments and other service personnel as it is for civvies.

For those of us who experience pain or physical limitations, it is very important to put something into our lives that will give us a sense of meaning and purpose; something that will give us direction. This is the secret of good mental health and was outlined in detail over 60 years ago by a psychotherapist called Viktor Frankl.

For you to gain maximum benefit from this section, it is set out for you in three simple steps. (Again, this is also another good between-session task.)

i.   What I have done in the past that has given me a sense of meaning and purpose in my life:

ii. What I am doing at present that gives me a sense of meaning and purpose in my life:

iii. What I will do over the next few months or years to give me an increased sense of meaning and purpose in my life:

...and my first small step will be:

...by when:

Beating Combat Stress: 101 Techniques for Recovery. By John Henden.
© 2011 John Wiley & Sons Ltd.

13. Keeping All Drugs at Bay

Many servicemen who have experienced some degree of battlefield stress will be using certain drugs to excess. It may be simply increased use of nicotine or a heavier reliance on alcohol. Some may be using over-the-counter drugs from the chemist and/or taking prescribed medication. Others will be using quantities of street drugs.

It is often seen as the easy option to increase drug intake as a way to soften the impact or give some relief from memories and experiences we would rather forget. Although this may help a little in the short term, in the long run *it does not work.*

Drug use – whether nicotine, alcohol, prescribed medication or street drugs – can cause other problems in both the medium and longer term. These can lead to serious life-threatening illnesses and premature death. Thousands of your predecessors have gone this way. Don't allow yourself to be one of these unnecessary statistics.

Welfare workers have a duty to inform personnel about the harmful effects of any form of drug use. There are dozens of excellent leaflets and pamphlets provided by many health promotion organisations and these should be given out, as appropriate.

There has been a lot of discussion recently about antidepressants and their effects on the brain. What we know

now is that most antidepressants only work in about 30% of cases after about six months; the idea of antidepressants "correcting the chemical imbalance in the brain" is now doubtful (Griffin and Tyrrell, 2004); and impotence is far more widespread than was first believed.

It is far better for health if we empower ourselves to take control by using methods involving the natural, God-given powers of mind and body. That is what this handbook is all about.

It is not helpful to beat ourselves up with this subject. Instead, we can ask ourselves solution-focused questions such as:

- "How has (alcohol/nicotine/the antidepressant, etc.) been helpful to me up to now?"
- "What have been the benefits of taking it?"
- "What have been the disadvantages of taking it?"
- "What else could I do differently to get similar relief?"
- "What might be the long-term benefits of taking this sort of action?"
- "How will I know when I am ready to have a conversation with the M.O. about reducing my drugs?"
- "As I begin to phase down my drug use, what side-effects will I notice becoming less?"
- "When I am off all drugs, or have got them down to a more satisfactory level, how will that be helpful to me?"
- "Once I am clear of all drugs, what will I notice about side-effects that I no longer have?"

Other important questions to answer:

i. **"What I have done so far to keep drink and all drugs at bay?"**

ii. **"What I will promise myself about keeping drink and drugs at bay over the next year?"**

iii. **Breaking this down into small, realistic, and achievable steps, these are:**

a.

b.

c.

d.

e.

Beating Combat Stress: 101 Techniques for Recovery. By John Henden.
© 2011 John Wiley & Sons Ltd.

14. Seek out Intimacy in Relationships

There is a basic human need for intimacy: either with a spouse, family members, buddies or close friends. This is not about sexual intimacy, but closeness and connectedness with those near and dear to us. Some people prefer the closeness of owning a cat, a dog, or another type of pet. This is okay, too.

As individuals, we feel more complete and fulfilled when intimacy plays an important part in our lives.

Considering ways in which this might be achieved can be both interesting and rewarding.

15. Reconnect with Yourself

This form of reconnection can often be achieved by spending time alone, by meditating, or by scribbling in a notebook or journal. It is about connecting deeply within the very core of our being: with our soul or spirit.

Ask yourself about your ideas on this; how it may have worked for you in the past; and how it might have been working for you recently. Once you have discovered what works or what helps, do more of it.

If this idea of reconnection with the self does not appeal to you, simply move on.

16. Reconnect to a Community

This again is a vital human need unless we are self-declared loners or hermits.

Connecting or reconnecting to the Regimental Association, veterans' organisation, another military support network, or an organisation for either serving or ex-serving can be of great benefit. It has even greater power when we become a net contributor to it. Similarly, connection to extended family, neighbourhood, church or community group can have similar value.

"Go national"

A young officer who had been medically discharged because of injuries received in combat, decided to join a nationwide federation of community family trusts that promoted initiatives for strengthening marriage and the family. He helped support marriage preparation courses and parenting classes in his particular town.

17. Connect to God or a "Higher Power"

A majority of people believe that we are more than simply mind and body: we have a spiritual aspect; there is a greater intelligence than ourselves, or a "higher being" at work in life. If you have a religious faith, you can develop your spiritual connectedness through prayer, services, meditation or study. Some seek conversion at this time. Throughout history, there have been many testimonies from people who have achieved great things through this form of connectedness. If you don't have this belief, you can still appeal to the massive creativity and healing power of nature itself.

My thoughts about this are:

18. Write a Letter to Someone You Really Admire

This exercise is a good one for those of us who need to "aim higher" with expectations both of ourselves now and what life might have ahead for us.

The instructions are as follows:

i.   Think of someone you really admire. This may be someone known to you (e.g., a mate, comrade, NCO or senior officer) or someone in the public eye.

ii. Imagine you are going to write a letter to this person outlining all the things you admire.

iii. Pick a quiet, private half-hour space and actively write the letter (which, of course, will not be sent).

The effects of writing such an imaginary letter are as follows:

- Qualities are flagged up that you would like to have more of yourself.
- Confidence and self-esteem levels are increased.

• There is a general increase in "the feel good factor".

19. Kick the "PTSD" Label into Touch

Some of our colleagues are pleased to announce that someone or other returning from a combat zone "has PTSD". Labels like this, however, are generally not helpful; and, for some, are seen as a life sentence. Their predecessors in years gone by used to issue other unhelpful labels. I have spent a lot of my recent career helping clients of all sorts work on their symptoms and remove these labels, so that they can resume living a full life, without them. A healthier and more positive way of looking at post-traumatic stress is to rename it "post-traumatic growth" (PTG) or "combat operational stress reaction" (COSR). These are both solution-focused terms.

If you or a buddy have been given the PTSD label, you have a wonderful opportunity to remove it or help him take it off. I will show how this can be achieved by the following example. The diagnosis, "has broken femur" requires certain procedures before the person can be declared "mobile again". There will be many stages, including "having bone re-set", "wound sewn together" and "plaster cast applied".

Similarly, dismantling the PTSD diagnostic label requires certain procedures. If (internal or external) triggers are identified, then you have tools and techniques available as described in Section 1. If flashbacks or other unwelcome thoughts are troublesome, then tools and techniques may be found in Sections 2 and 3. Any label can be limiting and handicapping, persuading the person to exist, rather than really to live. This section provides a whole range of strategies to encourage you to thrive, rather than simply to survive.

20. The Amazing Effect of the First Small Step

Sometimes we think about what we might like to do; what we would like to achieve in life. But doubts and fears can get in the way, sometimes, of our becoming the person we want to be.

The secret to making some headway in the right direction is to think what might be the first small step. Once you have done this, think of an *even smaller* step. Then, take it!

21. Don't Buy into the "Depression" Label

There are various definitions of depression and these can vary from practitioner to practitioner. Currently, my two preferred definitions are:

"Unexpressed emotion", or
"Undeclared or unresolved issues from the past".

Very recent brain research has questioned severely the traditional definition and treatment of depression.

Growing numbers of combatants and veterans can testify to the effectiveness of the tools and techniques within this handbook, in treating both depression and "the lows". This is achieved without resorting to chemicals; or, at most, using chemicals in the short term only.

Appendix A: The Evidence Base for Solution-focused Therapy

(I am indebted to Dr. Alasdair Macdonald for allowing me to draw information from his website for this Appendix)

Over the past 25 years or so, solution-focused therapy (SFT) applications, across many specialist areas, have been something of a mega-trend.

Eighty-nine relevant studies: two meta-analyses; three systematic reviews; 75 published follow-up studies; nine randomised controlled trials showing benefit from solution-focused brief therapy with six showing benefit over existing methods. Of 27 comparison studies, 21 favour SFT. Effectiveness data are available from more than 2900 cases with a success rate exceeding 60% and requiring an average of three to five sessions of therapy time. ("Solution focused" is the best keyword for Google searches.)

SFT is approved by the US Federal Government (www.samhsa.gov); State of Washington http://access.wa.gov; State of Oregon www.oregon.gov/DHS (C. Hansen, personal communication). Finland has a government-approved SFT accreditation programme. Canada has a registration body for solution-focused practitioners and therapists.

Also listed are two studies relating to domestic violence and three studies that are single-session follow-ups.

Beating Combat Stress: 101 Techniques for Recovery. By John Henden.
© 2011 John Wiley & Sons Ltd.

For links into other research and the evidence base for the effectiveness of the approach, the following websites will be of interest:

- European Brief Therapy Association (EBTA) homepage: www.ebta.nu
- SIKT homepage (www.sikt.nu)
- United Kingdom Association for Solution Focused Practice, *Solution News* (www.solution-news.co.uk; www.ukasfp.co.uk)
- SOLWorld (management) (www.solworld.org).

A. Meta-analyses

1. Kim, J.S. (2008) Examining the effectiveness of solution-focused brief therapy: a meta-analysis. *Research on Social Work Practice*, 18, 107–116.

Twenty-two studies; many factors examined. Small effects in favour of SFT; best for personal behaviour change, effect size estimate 0.26 (sig. $p < .05$). Thus SFT is equivalent to other therapies. (Dissertation: "Examining the effectiveness of solution-focused brief therapy: a meta-analysis using random effects modeling. University of Michigan database. Up to 6.5 sessions required. Competence in SFT requires >20 hours of training?)

2. Stams, G.J., Dekovic, M., Buist, K, and de Vries, L. (2006) Effectiviteit van oplossingsgerichte korte therapie: een meta-analyse (Efficacy of solution focused brief therapy: a meta-analysis). *Gedragstherapie*, 39 (2), 81–95. (Dutch; abstract in English).

Twenty-one studies; many factors examined. Small to moderate effect: better than no treatment; as good as other treatments. Best results for personal behaviour change, adults, residential or group settings. Recent studies show strongest effects. Shorter than other therapies; respects client autonomy.

B. Systematic Reviews

1. Corcoran, J. and Pillai, V. (2007) A review of the research on solution-focused therapy. *British Journal of Social Work*, 10, 1–9.

Ten quasi-experimental studies, all in English, included on the basis of statistics/design/ follow-up/ numbers. Only two follow-up studies. Moderate or high effect size in four studies. Are qualified workers better than students?

2. Gingerich, W.J. and Eisengart, S. (2000) Solution focused brief therapy: a review of the outcome research. *Family Process*, 39, 477–498.

Fifteen outcome studies: five strong, four moderately strong, six weak (updated version: www.gingerich.net).

3. Kim, J.S. and Franklin, C. (2009) Solution-focused brief therapy in schools: a review of the outcome literature. *Children and Youth Services Review*, 31 (4), 464–470.

An extension of Kim (2008) examining seven studies of SFT in school settings. This review suggest that SFT may be effectively applied with at-risk students in a school setting, specifically helping to reduce the intensity of negative feelings and to manage conduct problems and externalising behavioural problems. Age ranges for applications in schools appeared flexible, from 5th graders to older children and adolescents.

C. Published Follow-up Studies

Please refer to Alasdair Macdonald's website (www.solutionsdoc.co.uk) for information on these.

D. Randomised Controlled Studies

1. Cockburn, J.T., Thomas, F.N. and Cockburn, O.J. (1997) Solution-focused therapy and psychosocial adjustment to orthopedic rehabilitation in a work hardening program. Journal *of Occupational Rehabilitation*, 7, 97–106.

Twenty-nine experimental: 6 SFT sessions versus 23 controls: standard rehabilitation. Sixty-eight per cent experimental at work within seven days at 60-day follow-up versus 4% controls.

2. Froeschle, J.G., Smith, R.L. and Ricard, R. (2007) The Efficacy of a Systematic Substance Abuse Program for Adolescent Females. *Professional School Counseling*, 10, 498–505.

Thirty-two experimental versus 33 controls; pre-test post-test design. Sixteen weekly SFT group/action learning/mentoring. Drug use, attitudes to use, knowledge of drugs, home and school behaviour all improved significantly.

3. Knekt, P. and Lindfors, O. (2004) A randomised trial of the effect of four forms of psychotherapy on depressive and anxiety disorders: design, methods and results on the effectiveness of short-term psychodynamic psychotherapy and solution-focused therapy during a one-year follow-up. *Studies in Social Security and Health*, 77, Social Insurance Institution, Helsinki, Finland.

Randomised comparison study; 93 SFT versus 98 short-term psychotherapy; problems >1 year. SFT 43% (mood), 26% (anxiety) recovery at 7 months maintained at 12 months; short-term 43%, 35%; no significant difference between therapies but SFT faster for depression; short-term better for "personality disorder". Average SFT 10 sessions over 7.5 months; short-term 15 sessions over 5.7 months. No figures for partial recovery; no apparent social class difference. At three-year follow-up gains maintained with long-term psychotherapy only. (Unpublished: one SFT rehospitalised versus five from short-term and six from long-term psychotherapy.) Psychoanalysis comparison data not yet published.

4. Knekt, P., Lindfors, O., Härkänen, T. *et al.* (2008) Randomised trial on the effectiveness of long- and short-term psychodynamic psychotherapy and solution-focused

therapy on psychiatric symptoms during a three-year follow-up. *Psychological Medicine*, 38, 689–703).

5. Lindforss, L., Magnusson, D. (1997) Solution-focused therapy in prison. *Contemporary Family Therapy*, 19, 89–104.

Two randomised studies: (1) Pilot study 14/21 (66%) experimental and 19/21 (90%) controls reoffended at 20 months. (2) 30 experimental and 29 controls; 16-month follow-up. Eighteen (60%) reoffended in experimental group, 25 (86%) in control; more drug offences and more total offences in control. Average five sessions; 2.7 million Swedish crowns saved by reduced reoffending.

6. Nystuen, P. and Hagen, K.B. (2006) Solution-focused intervention for sick listed employees with psychological problems or muscle skeletal pain: a randomised controlled trial. *BMC Public Health*, 6, 69 –77.

Long-term sickness; randomised; 53 experimental versus 50 controls; eight sessions; one-year follow-up. No significant difference in return to work; mental health scores significantly improved. Authors question sample size and chosen measures.

7. Smock, S.A., Trepper, T.S., Wetchler, J.L. *et al.* (2008) Solution-focused group therapy for level 1 substance abusers. *Journal of Marital and Family Therapy*, 34 (1),107–120.

Randomised; 27 experimental; six-weekly groups; 29 control; six-weekly Hazelden program groups. 19 experimental, 19 control completed; significant improvement in depression and symptom distress; dependence scores unchanged. No follow-up.

8. Thorslund, K.W. (2007) Solution-focused group therapy for patients on long-term sick leave: a comparative outcome study. *Journal of Family Psychotherapy*, 18 (3),11–24.

Randomised; 15 experimental, 15 control; one to five months sick. Eight sessions; increased return to work (60%, 9, versus 13%, 2) and psychological health improved at three-month follow-up.

9. Wilmshurst, L.A. (2002) Treatment programs for youth with emotional and behavioural disorders: an outcome study of two alternate approaches. *Mental Health Services Research*, 4, 85–96.

Randomised controlled study; 12 weeks; 27 clients, five day a week residential, SFT, family contact 26 hours; 38 non-resident programme, cognitive behavioural therapy (CBT), family contact 48 hours. One-year follow-up: behaviour improved in both groups; attention-deficit hyperactivity disorder (ADHD) behaviours better in 63% of CBT, 22% of SFT; group scores better for anxiety and depression with CBT. Author suggests residential care is detrimental.

E. Domestic Violence Studies

1. Georgiades, S.D. (2008) A solution-focused intervention with a youth in a domestic violence situation: longitudinal evidence. *Contemporary Family Therapy*, 30 (3), 141–151.

Abstract: This article reports on a four-year therapeutic intervention combining in-person and email communication with a 13-year-old Greek-Cypriot teenager who witnessed and later was the victim of severe domestic violence. The intervention is based on an empowerment philosophy and solution-focused strategies, and its usefulness is evaluated by three standardised measures at five time points between the years 1999 and 2003. Pertinent cultural and ethical dynamics of the interventional context are highlighted. The intervention may have helped to produce better perpetrator–youth relations, remission of the client's depression and post-traumatic stress symptoms, and improvement in his academic performance. Implications and limitations are discussed.

2. McNamara, J.R., Tamanini, K. and Pelletier-Walker, S. (2008) The impact of short-term counseling at a domestic violence shelter. *Research on Social Work Practice*.

Objective: Women who received counselling at a domestic violence shelter were evaluated with several measures to determine the impact of the services they received. Method: A pre-test and post-test design using clinical measures for life functioning and coping ability, along with post-test (only) measures of satisfaction and helpfulness of service, were used to assess the outcomes of the counselling and other social work services at the agency. Results: significant improvement on clinical measures of life functioning as well as, along with a sense of being helped and satisfied with the social work services received are noted. Conclusions: counselling, along with, proves beneficial to women seeking services for Pre-post only; no controls.

F. Single-session Studies

1. Lamprecht, H., Laydon, C. and McQuillan, C. *et al.* (2007) Single-session solution-focused brief therapy and self-harm: a pilot study. *Journal of Psychiatric and Mental Health Nursing*, 14, 601–602.

Forty first-time self-harmers; one session. Two repeat (6.25%) in one-year follow-up versus 40/302 (13.2%) untreated (updates Wiseman, 2003, see below). Brief intervention: reducing the repetition of deliberate self-harm. *Nursing Times*, 99, 34–36).

2. Perkins. R. (2006) The effectiveness of one session of therapy using a single-session therapy approach for children and adolescents with mental health problems. *Psychology and Psychotherapy: Theory, Research and Practice*, 79, 215–227.

Seventy-eight experimental single session, 88 no treatment; follow-up 4 weeks. Severity improved 74.3% versus 42.5%; frequency improved 71.45% versus 48.3%.

3. Wiseman, S. (2003) Brief intervention: reducing the repetition of deliberate self-harm. *Nursing Times*, 99, 34–36.

First self-harm 40 clients; one session. Up to six months follow-up: 39 (97%) no repeat; 78% improved on self-scaling.

Appendix B: Helpful Questions and Statements from the Worker

From extensive and varied experience in doing this valuable work, the following questions and statements have been found to be most useful and helpful:

1) "How much of the detail do you need to tell me before you are ready to move on?"
2) "What do you think your significant others (friends, boss, etc.) will begin to notice about you as you sort things out in your own mind and move forward even more?"
3) "What strengths, qualities or special abilities did you call into play to survive that time or those incidents?"
4) "What have you done, up to now, not only to sort things out in your own mind, but to live your life well or as well as possible?"
5) "How would you like to use these sessions?"
6) "What do you feel you need to tell me, in order for me to be most helpful to you?"
7) "What particular techniques do you use to counteract any unwelcome thoughts you might be having?"
8) "On a scale of 1–10, where are you now, in terms of living your life well?"
9) "What we know from this type of work is that people can work through things which might hold them back."
10) "It is quite common for people to feel guilty at surviving an incident in theatre."

Beating Combat Stress: 101 Techniques for Recovery. By John Henden.
© 2011 John Wiley & Sons Ltd.

11) "What has been particularly helpful to you so far in expressing your anger in safe ways?"

12) "What particular strengths, qualities, resources do you have that you have found to be helpful in the past; and which could be useful to you in the months and years to come?"

13) "What would be the first (smallest) sign that things are getting better, that this incident is having less of an impact on your life?"

14) "What will you be doing differently when this (the incident) is less of a problem in your life?"

15) "What will you be doing differently with your time?"

16) "What useful things will you be in the habit of saying to yourself?"

17) "What will you be thinking about (doing) **instead** of the thinking about the past?"

18) "Tell me about some times when the above is happening to some (even small) extent, already."

19) "What difference will the above healing changes make when they have been present in your life over an extended period of time (weeks, days, months, years)?"

20) "What do you think that your (significant other) would say would be the first sign that things are getting better?" "What do you think that person would notice first?"

Appendix C: What Service Users Have Found to be Helpful in This Work

Service users found it helpful when people:

- enabled identification of conflicts they were experiencing or feeling
- encouraged working through these issues, if that was what they wanted
- promoted self-esteem and self-confidence
- encouraged them to take control of their lives
- allowed them to choose the goals of therapy, in accordance with their wishes and values
- maximised collaboration; minimised resistance in the work
- encouraged them to give up secrecy and shame in their lives
- gave information: both verbal and written
- provided a good quality therapeutic relationship for disclosing: this mobilised their capacity for self-healing and growth
- built a trusting relationship
- provided acceptance, and supported and encouraged them to confront conflicts where appropriate
- helped them to share thoughts and feelings
- showed understanding
- gave time

Beating Combat Stress: 101 Techniques for Recovery. By John Henden.
© 2011 John Wiley & Sons Ltd.

- enabled correct apportionment of blame
- acknowledged, validated and normalised thoughts and feelings wherever possible
- helped them to express emotions, thoughts and feelings
- simply allowed them to disclose or divulge what happened in their own way
- asked what they were seeking in treatment and how they would know when treatment had been successful
- did not assume that they needed to go back and work through traumatic memories (some do, some don't)
- made provisions (e.g., contracts), on occasions as necessary, for safety from suicide, homicide and other potentially dangerous situations (it was best when these were mutual)
- remained focused on the goals of treatment, rather than getting lost in the gory details
- did not give the message that they were "damaged goods" or that their future was determined by having experienced the traumatic or stressful incident
- admitted sometimes to getting it wrong
- enabled them to feel safe.

Appendix D: How to Avoid Re-traumatisation and Re-victimisation

The following eight tips have proved invaluable in helping workers do this important work both successfully and in a helpful way for ex-servicemen.

1. Show compassion and deep empathy.
2. As the service user discloses, acknowledge, validate and normalise all feelings and sensations expressed.
3. Ask the following strength-based questions, interrupting as appropriate while the service user is disclosing:
   - How did you cope at the time?
     - What got you through all this?
     - What helped most?
     - How did you do that?
     - How did you know how to do that?
   - Looking back on what happened, in what ways has it made you a more determined and stronger person?
   - Awful though it was, which aspects of surviving it have made you a better person?
4. It is important to compliment sincerely, where appropriate, both as the service user is disclosing and, most importantly, at the end of the session.

Beating Combat Stress: 101 Techniques for Recovery. By John Henden.
© 2011 John Wiley & Sons Ltd.

5. Treat the content with care, respect and in a supportive manner.
6. Value and affirm, verbally and non-verbally.
7. Keep your own and your service user's eyes on the treatment goals.
8. Keep to "the five o'clock rule" (see Henden, 2008).

Appendix E: Blocks to Disclosing

Below is a fairly comprehensive list of the main "blocks" service personnel and veterans have in speaking to a welfare worker or other professional. With some of these, the potential service user simply will not come forward at all. A large number who do come forward will not talk much because one or several of these blocks get in the way. If you can identify the block or blocks with the service user, you may be able to help them remove it or get past it, so they can move forward.

Gender of worker

Guilt

Shame

Concerns about Official Secrets

Not being believed

Fear of rejection

Fear of consequences

Fear of Chain of Command finding out

Loss of control

Special needs disability

Rank or perceived status of worker

Having been told by officers or NCOs to "button it"

Inarticulation

Denial

Feeling unsafe

Feeling contaminated by war and therefore not wanting to infect or affect worker

Not wanting to be seen in poor light by worker

Embarrassment

Religious beliefs

Previous poor experiences when disclosing

Fear of being judged

Not trusting the environment (answer-phone for messages, paper-thin walls, too many windows, etc.)

Believing the worker's knowledge of the subject is insufficient

Fear of being seen as weak/soft/not able to cope

Non-recognition

Worker perceived as not understanding military context

Reaction of worker unsure

Inexperience of worker

Betrayal of comrades

Civvy status of worker

Worker too young

Fear of being seen going to welfare or neighbours seeing welfare worker arrive

Lack of trust

Appendix F: The Three Stages: Victim – Survivor – Thriver (Living Life to the Full, or as Full as Possible)[1]

Information for Service Users

Victim

- First stage of healing. It is important for you to face the reality of the bad or unfortunate thing that happened.
- You can then acknowledge the negative feelings and emotions that might be around (grief, anger, sadness, disappointment, frustration, despair, hopelessness, helplessness, etc.)
- Allow yourself to experience these feelings and emotions: and to express them.
- This is a vital part of healing and a valuable part of this stage.
- It is also important to recognise that what happened **was not your fault**, so you can let go of self-blame and shame. (In the small number of cases where it was partly your fault, it is important for you to attribute only the correct proportion of blame to yourself. Then, it is important for you to

[1]With full acknowledgement to Yvonne Dolan for the original version. Handout developed from ideas outlined by Yvonne Dolan in her book, *Beyond Survival: Living Well is the Best Revenge* (BT Press, 2000).

Beating Combat Stress: 101 Techniques for Recovery. By John Henden.
© 2011 John Wiley & Sons Ltd.

consider in what ways, constructively, you may make amends for what occurred.)

- Find the courage to tell someone else what happened to you; this breaks down the isolation.
- As soon as the victim stage has been acknowledged and understood, you can move into the next stage – survivor.

Survivor

- This begins when you understand you have lived beyond the traumatic or highly stressful experience(s) that occurred.
- This stage reinforces the fact that it happened in the past.
- Then questions may be asked: "How did I survive it?" "How did I do it?" and "What strengths and resources did I use?"
- Acknowledgment of survivor-hood involves:
  - developing an inventory of positive personality characteristics
  - identifying and appreciating the internal strengths (knowledge, courage, spirituality and other positive aspects of self), which have got you this far.
  - identifying external resources: mates, Chain of Command, padre, welfare, supportive family members, community support, etc. – at the time of the incident(s) and afterwards.
- At this stage you will regain ability to function in everyday life: work, family time, household chores, time with mates, hobbies, community activities, etc.
- *Once you have acknowledged you've survived, and the skills, strengths, qualities and resources that have got you to survival and eventual wellbeing, move on – to thriving; move on – to live life to the full and to live as purposeful and meaningful a life as possible.*

Thriver – Living Life to the Full

- This allows you more freedom than the earlier stages.
- It allows you to experience a more compelling present and to contemplate a future that is more vivid and fulfilling than your past.
- It is now possible to enjoy life to the fullest, within any physical limitations you may have.
- It is worthwhile to explore possibilities and dreams for the future that you may be having right now.
- It is now possible for you to express yourself in the most personally rewarding and creative ways available to you.
- In this stage, your current experiences and relationships may evoke increasingly a sense of immediacy, wonder and enhanced potential for future growth.

Appendix G: Benefits of Doing This Important Work

Whether you are a serviceman, veteran or welfare worker, this comprehensive list outlines the countless benefits to be gained by getting stuck in to this useful work. What's stopping you? What's your next small step?

No to:	Yes to:
Life of fear and anxiety	Successful personal relationships
Marital or couple break-up	Quality family life
Existence as a victim or survivor	Passing on tips and techniques to other survivors
Constant pulling around the PTSD ball and chain	Living life well
Excessive use of drink, drugs or tobacco to cope	Healthy living and eating
Feeling out of control	Feeling in control; living life well
Finding difficulty resting or doing nothing in particular	Physical fitness, as much as possible
Feelings of "stuckness"	Feelings of great joy, from time to time

Beating Combat Stress: 101 Techniques for Recovery. By John Henden.
© 2011 John Wiley & Sons Ltd.

No to:	**Yes to:**
Fearful of unexpected triggers	Welcoming triggers on which to practise techniques learned
Difficulties with everyday functioning	Getting on well with day-to-day tasks
Feeling that life is meaningless and pointless	Having a sense of meaning and purpose in life
Disturbed sleep, with recurrent nightmares	Settled sleep patterns
Feeling odd and disconnected from people	Enjoying a connectedness with people – especially loved ones
Reliving, constantly, what happened	Regarding what happened as being part of life, but not being dominated by it.
General unhappiness and discontentedness with life	Personal goals and targets in life to look forward to
Sudden and unpredictable outbursts of anger	Safely controlled aggression
Isolating self excessively from family and friends, in particular	Having a forward view of life, in terms of chapters yet to be written

Appendix H: Reassuring Things for Servicemen to Know

1. Not everyone who experiences a traumatic incident will develop combat operational stress reaction (COSR). In fact, the figure is around only 10–15%.
2. There are both positive and negative effects from operational stress.
3. If COSR is experienced, you don't have to go for trauma therapy from an "expert professional". Self-help and "buddy-aid" are sufficient in most cases.
4. Getting help does not mean you are weak. It takes great courage to meet up, in confidence, with a complete stranger, to talk through your experiences.
5. With COSR, when meeting up with a welfare worker, you don't have to go over everything or remember all that happened. Meeting a welfare worker does not mean you are going barmy and should lose your place in the military.
6. Symptoms of COSR can be dealt with simply and effectively in the short term – without the use of over-medication, depth psychology or long-term psychotherapy.
7. Buying into "a PTSD diagnosis", with its long-term implications, generally, is unhelpful.
8. You can find freedom from symptoms without resorting to the often mind-numbing and/or anxiety-provoking side

Beating Combat Stress: 101 Techniques for Recovery. By John Henden.
© 2011 John Wiley & Sons Ltd.

effects of psychotropic drugs such as citalopram, paroxetine, tryptophan and fluoxetine. Prescribed drugs often promise freedom but, quite commonly, their side effects reduce it or take it away. (It is fair to say some have found them helpful in the short term, but rarely in the long term.)

9. An achievable and realistic aim of recovering from COSR is a happier, more fulfilled, meaningful, peaceful and joyous life.

Appendix I: Two-day Workshops

These two-day workshops, dealing with combat operational stress reaction (COSR), have been running for some years. In addition, two-day workshops dealing with severe trauma and stress, generally, are delivered to a wide range of organisations.

The workshop content and learning objectives are outlined below:

Workshop Content

- Welcome and introductions
- Contracting around making it safe for people to work
- Aims and objectives
- Outline plan for the two days
- The solution-focused approach
- Scaling confidence
- Other trauma: RTAs, robberies, muggings, near-death experiences and terrorist attacks
- What has been found to have worked in one-to-one work with survivors
- What service users have found helpful

Beating Combat Stress: 101 Techniques for Recovery. By John Henden.
© 2011 John Wiley & Sons Ltd.

- The three stages: "victim"; "survivor"; "thriver"
- The basic tools and techniques of solution-focused brief therapy (SFBT)
- Survival skills outlined
- Dealing with anger and "the solution-focused feelings tank"
- Applying basic SFBT techniques to survivors
- Sticking to "the five o'clock rule"
- Disclosing or divulging what happened
- The detail: how much is necessary to know?
- Blocks to disclosing
- What equips us to do this work?
- Introducing specialised techniques
- Implications of this type of work for workers and how they can look after themselves
- Getting to know the "thriver"
- The specialised techniques:
    ◦ "Let it go ... Let it go ... Let it go"
    ◦ The "Stop!" technique and "replaying the DVD" later
    ◦ "That was then, this is NOW ... !"
    ◦ "Dual awareness" for dealing with intrusive thoughts
    ◦ The "Rainy Day Letter"
    ◦ Letter from the future and how to use it
    ◦ "Park it ... and move on"
    ◦ The solution-focused feelings tank
    ◦ Fast-forwarding the DVD of your life
    ◦ Write, read and shred or burn
    ◦ "Shrinking" for dealing with flashbacks
    ◦ Dealing with "the lows"
- Purpose and meaning in life, or Living life as full as possible
- How we can improve further our practice, from today
- Workshop roundup or summary
- Recommended reading list

- Workshop evaluation
- Presentation of certificates

Learning Outcomes

At the end of the workshop, attendees will be able to:

- demonstrate an increased understanding of COSR
- describe the characteristics of the "victimhood", "survivorhood" and "thriverhood" ("living life well")
- describe the basic SFBT tools and techniques used with service personnel
- use a variety of specialised tools and techniques for helping personnel move further towards thriverhood/living life well/ their authentic selves
- recognise how the specialised techniques can be applied to other types of potentially traumatic situation
- list the main points personnel have made about how welfare workers can best be helpful
- name the pitfalls when working with COSR and/or other types of trauma
- highlight the most helpful and useful questions to ask personnel
- list the key ways welfare workers can look after themselves to enable them to undertake this important work
- feel more confident in their work with a wide range of personnel who have experienced COSR and other types of trauma.

Bibliography

American Psychiatric Association (APA) (2000) *Diagnostic and Statistical Manual of Mental Disorders*, 2nd edn, text revision (DSM-IV-TR), Washington DC: APA.

Armstrong, K., Best, S. and Domenici, P. (2006) *Courage after Fire: Coping Strategies for Troops Returning from Iraq and Afghanistan and Their Families*, Ulysses Press, Berkeley, California.

Capacchione, L. (1979) *The Creative Journal: The Art of Finding Yourself*, University/Swallow Press, Ohio.

Coleman, V. (1994) *Know Your Drugs*, European Medical Journal.

Coleman, V. (2001) *How to Live Longer (and Look and Feel Younger)*, European Medical Journal.

Davies, M. (2006) *Sod It! The Depression 'Virus' and How to Deal with it*, Sod-It! Books.

Davies, M. (2007) *Sod It All! How to Deal with the Stress Virus in Your Life*, Sod-It! Books.

Dolan, Y. (2000) *Beyond Survival: Living Well is the Best Revenge*, BT Press, London.

Frankl, V.E. (1964) *Man's Search for Meaning: An Introduction to Logotherapy*, Hodder & Stoughton, Ltd., London.

Frankl, V.E. (1967) *Psychotherapy and Existentialism: Selected Papers on Logotherapy*, Pelican Books.

Frankl, V.E. (1979) *The Unheard Cry for Meaning*. Hodder & Stoughton, Ltd., London.

Furman, B. (1997) *It's Never Too Late to have a Happy Childhood: From Adversity to Resilience*, BT Press, London.

Beating Combat Stress: 101 Techniques for Recovery. By John Henden.
© 2011 John Wiley & Sons Ltd.

Grenier, S., Darte, K., Heber, A. and Richardson, D. (2007) The operational stress injury social support program: a peer support program in collaboration between the Canadian forces and veterans' affairs Canada, in *Combat Stress Injury: Theory, Research and Management* (eds C.R. Figley and W.P. Nash), Routledge.

Griffin, J. and Tyrrell, I. (2004) *Human Givens: A New Approach to Emotional Health and Clear Thinking*. Human Givens Publishing.

Hartman, R.J. (2008) *PTSD 2008: Are We Ready to Serve Our Troops?* iUniverse, Inc.

Henden, J. (2008) *Preventing Suicide: The Solution Focused Approach*. John Wiley & Sons, Ltd.

Hoge, C.W. (2010) *Once a Warrior, Always a Warrior: Navigating the Transition from Combat to Home*, GPP Life, Guilford, Connecticut.

Jacob, F. (2001) *Solution Focused Recovery from Eating Distress*, BT Press, London.

McManners, H. (1993) *The Scars of War*, HarperCollins Publishers, Denver, Colorado.

Moore, B.A. and Reger, G.M. (2007) Historical and contemporary perspectives of combat stress and the army combat stress control team, in *Combat Stress Injury: Theory, Research and Management* (eds C.R. Figley and W.P. Nash), Routledge.

Paulson, D.S. and Krippner, S. (2007) *Haunted by Combat: Understanding PTSD in War Veterans Including Women Reservists, and Those Coming Back from Iraq*, Praeger Publishers.

Rothschild, B. (2003) *The Body Remembers Casebook: Unifying Methods and Models in the Treatment of Trauma and PTSD*, W.W. Norton, New York.

Ruben, D.H. (2008) *The Human War: PTSD Recovery Guide for Returning Soldiers*, Outskirts Press, Denver, Colorado.

Shephard, B. (2002) *A War of Nerves: Soldiers and Psychiatrists 1914–1994*, Pimlico Books, London.

Useful websites

Frank Gardner, http://en.wikipedia.org/wiki/Frank_Gardner_
(journalist)
Phil Packer, www.philpacker.com
Simon Weston, www.simonweston.com
Solution-focused approaches, www.solutionsdoc.co.uk
What is the Diaphragm Muscle? www.wisegeek.com/what-is-the-
diaphragm-muscle.htm

Index